¡ Dios te bendiga siempre !

180
PRAYERS
~ for a ~
# GIRL OF
# GOD

Oniki,
Abri te ama
con todo el
corazón.

iembre
2019

D0596875

Compiled and edited by JoAnne Simmons

ISBN 978-1-68322-708-3

Published by Barbour Books, an imprint of Barbour Publishing, Inc., 1810 Barbour Drive, Uhrichsville, Ohio 44683, www.barbourbooks.com

Our mission is to inspire the world with the life-changing message of the Bible.

Member of the
Evangelical Christian
Publishers Association

Printed in the United States of America.

06200 0918 DP

180
PRAYERS
~ for a ~
GIRL OF
GOD

BARBOUR BOOKS
An Imprint of Barbour Publishing, Inc.

INTRODUCTION

"Never stop praying," says God's Word in 1 Thessalonians 5:17 (NLT). What a short and sweet scripture (you can memorize it, easy-peasy), yet it's packed with incredible power! The amazing Creator, the one true God of the entire universe wants to stay in *constant* communication with you. Why? Because He loves you like crazy and sent His Son, Jesus, to live and die and rise again to make a way for you to have relationship with Him. He wants to help you with everything in order for you to live the very best kind of life, not just here on earth but for eternity too. I hope you realize how awesome that is! Because of Jesus, you can talk to God about absolutely anything. Nothing is off-limits. He cares, and He wants to hear from you endlessly. Let these 180 prayers encourage and inspire you, and then don't stop there—continue on in lifelong, nonstop prayer!

PRAYER

Father, You are the best listener in my life! But I often forget to take advantage of Your listening ear. I run to my mom or my best friend and completely forget to pour my troubles out to You. Thank You for providing me with people in my life whom I can talk to about things, but help me to remember that You want to hear about things too.

I forget that prayer can be a conversation. I need to listen for You. You may not say anything, but You do make Yourself heard in my life. I can talk to You anywhere, anytime. Thank You for Your constantly listening ear and for all the ways that You encourage me and are patient with me. Amen.

*Each morning you listen
to my prayer, as I bring my
requests to you and wait for your reply.*
PSALM 5:3 CEV

YOUR PLAN FOR MY LIFE

Dear God, I spend a lot of time thinking about what my life will look like in the future. Right now it's pretty basic: I go to school, I spend time with my friends and family, and extracurricular and church activities take up the rest of my time. But I wonder what happens when I'm done with school and I no longer live with my family—what will my life look like then? Help me to trust Your will and Your plans. You already know what I will do in the next fifty years, even though I have no idea. That's so crazy to think about! Thank You! Help me to trust Your words and to listen for Your voice when I'm making big decisions. Amen.

For you created my inmost being;
you knit me together in my mother's womb.
PSALM 139:13 NIV

A GOOD MODEL

Father, I pray that You would provide good role models for me throughout my lifetime. Please give me wisdom about whom I look up to as I get older. Help me to be careful about whom I trust and whom I allow into my heart.

Help me to understand that not everyone who claims to be a Christian has a true relationship with You. I pray You would give me the ability to understand right from wrong and to be able to tell when someone is true or fake. Amen.

༺ঌ

Join together in following my example, brothers and sisters, and just as you have us as a model, keep your eyes on those who live as we do.
PHILIPPIANS 3:17 NIV

YOUR INSTRUCTION BOOK

Lord, I'm sorry that I don't always treat Your Word with the value it deserves—it sometimes stays unopened as I try to find my way through life on my own. But You have given Your Word so that I can learn from the mistakes of people who have messed up, as well as learn from the good choices others have made in doing things Your way. I can read about how much You love me and forgive me as well as what I need to do to act and live wisely.

God, thank You for sharing Your "instruction manual" with me! Amen.

❧

All Scripture is inspired by God and is useful to teach us what is true and to make us realize what is wrong in our lives. It corrects us when we are wrong and teaches us to do what is right.
2 TIMOTHY 3:16 NLT

NOWHERE TO RUN

God, You know *everything* about me? That's a scary thought! But when I consider that You know and yet still love me, that wraps around me like a warm blanket. I don't have to pretend anything with You. (You already know anyway!) It's wonderful to have a Friend who can understand me better than I understand myself.

There is nowhere I can go to get away from Your presence. Ever. A love so deep and strong is impossible for me to grasp. Help remind me of that, Lord, when I am filled with doubts about being loved. Amen.

*O Lord, you have examined my
heart and know everything about me.
You know when I sit down or stand up.
You know my thoughts even when I'm far away.*
Psalm 139:1–2 nlt

JOY VS. HAPPINESS

Father, help me to remember the difference between happiness and joy. At times I think the words mean the same thing, but they really don't. Happiness is a result of what happens to and around me. But joy—*true* joy—comes from knowing that You love me so much and care about what happens to me. So even on the absolute worst of days, I can still have joy in my heart because I have You in and with me.

I want to live a life full of joy, Jesus, and want others to see that I'm different. Because even when bad things happen, I can still have a spirit of joy and rest in Your goodness. Amen.

❧

*Therefore my heart is glad and my tongue
rejoices; my body also will rest secure.*
PSALM 16:9 NIV

THE BEST BOOK OF ALL

Reading a good book is so much fun, Lord, but I thank You, Father, for the best book of all—one loaded with more adventure, more history, and more personal stories than any other. Your Word—the Bible—is action-packed! Wow! I learn so much when I take the time to read it. Remind me every day how important it is to read this amazing book and to pray for those who haven't had a chance to read it yet. I can't wait to see what happens next, Lord! Amen.

"Keep this Book of the Law always on your lips; meditate on it day and night, so that you may be careful to do everything written in it. Then you will be prosperous and successful."
JOSHUA 1:8 NIV

THE BEAUTY OF THE HEART

Heavenly Father, Your Word says that You look at our hearts to determine our beauty. It is much more important who I am on the inside than what I look like on the outside.

I ask You to give me confidence in who I am as Your daughter. Help me to believe that I am beautiful just as You made me and that I do not need to add a lot of "extras" to my appearance. Amen.

∽

Your beauty should not come from outward adornment, such as elaborate hairstyles and the wearing of gold jewelry or fine clothes. Rather, it should be that of your inner self, the unfading beauty of a gentle and quiet spirit, which is of great worth in God's sight.
1 PETER 3:3–4 NIV

TRUE SUCCESS

I want to know You more, Father God. I want to be successful not only in my physical life but in my spiritual life as well. I want You first in my life because that's true success. You said to seek the kingdom of God and Your righteousness, and everything else will fall into place!

Please nudge me to read the Bible and spend time with You every day, Lord, before I do anything else. So many things draw me away from quiet time with You. I desire to seek You with all of my heart. And I know that if I do, You will take care of all the other needs in my life. Amen.

"But seek first the kingdom of God and His righteousness, and all these things shall be added to you."
MATTHEW 6:33 NKJV

LIVING THE FAITH

"Would I be happy if someone did this to me?" Lord, help me to focus on that question every time I do anything to—or for—another person. Let my actions show that I love You. Help me to be the kind of girl that not only talks about my faith in You but lives it!

There are a lot of girls that don't really care about other people's feelings. They've said things about me and my friends that hurt! Help me to remember that deep inside they are longing for the love that only You can give. Help me to share Your love with them, even if I don't feel like it at the time. Amen.

"Do to others whatever you would like them to do to you. This is the essence of all that is taught in the law and the prophets."
MATTHEW 7:12 NLT

A FOREVER HOME

Dear God, heaven must be an awesome place. Some people say that everyone goes to heaven, but the Bible tells me that only those who know You and have their sins forgiven will be there. Help me to remember that eternity is more important than this world. I don't know how long my life will last here, but eternity doesn't end. I want my friends and family to be there with me, God. Show me how to tell them about You so they can be ready to meet You someday. Amen.

"There is more than enough room in my Father's home. If this were not so, would I have told you that I am going to prepare a place for you? When everything is ready, I will come and get you, so that you will always be with me where I am."
JOHN 14:2–3 NLT

FROM SORROW TO JOY

I'm really down, Father. I seem to have no hope. I have lost someone close to me, and I don't know when things will be the same again. Some days I feel so sad that I don't know what to do.

Open Your Word to me. Lead me to a new hope. Give me the courage to keep going. Lift the weight of sorrow from my heart. Help me to take things one moment, one hour, one day at a time, knowing that You are holding my hand through it all. Show me how to praise You, for I know that when I do, I will feel better. Amen.

I would have lost heart, unless I had believed that I would see the goodness of the LORD in the land of the living.
PSALM 27:13 NKJV

THE INSIDE RATHER THAN THE OUTSIDE

Father, I can relate to David, the shepherd boy whom Jesse had not even bothered to call in from the field. No one imagined David would be chosen. No one ever seems to notice me either. I just feel really *average* sometimes, like there is nothing outstanding about me. The story of David is a great reminder that You use regular people—sometimes even those whom no one would suspect—to do special things in Your kingdom! When You look at my heart, I pray that You will find me faithful and ready to serve. Amen.

But the LORD said to Samuel, "Do not consider his appearance or his height, for I have rejected him. The LORD does not look at the things people look at. People look at the outward appearance, but the LORD looks at the heart."
1 SAMUEL 16:7 NIV

THOUGHTS

Lord, I know thoughts can be very powerful. So, please, Lord, help me to keep a positive attitude. Help me to think of good things. Plant Your Word in me so that I will keep in mind all the things You say are important—loving others (even enemies), obeying my parents, being kind to everyone, forgiving people (including myself), taking care of my body, and being content in every situation. Help me to make Your Word my word, in all I do and say. Build me up within to look on the bright side no matter what is happening on the outside. Each day give me a new heart and mind focused on Your Light. Amen.

For as he thinks in his heart, so is he.
PROVERBS 23:7 NKJV

THE GIFT OF FRIENDSHIP

Dear God, thank You for the friends You have given me. I pray that You would continue to bless all of my friendships. Sometimes it's hard to be a good friend; it's easier to be selfish and concentrate on what makes me happy or what I want to do. Help me to remember to put others first and to settle any disagreements with kindness and gentleness. I want to be a good friend and show them how much I care. Thank You for being the perfect example of a friend who loves at all times. Amen.

But the wisdom from above is first of all pure. It is also peace loving, gentle at all times, and willing to yield to others. It is full of mercy and the fruit of good deeds. It shows no favoritism and is always sincere.
JAMES 3:17 NLT

A WAY OUT

Every day, Lord, I face a ton of temptations. All of them could get really overwhelming if I didn't realize I have You to help me overcome them. Thank You that I'm not alone. Lots of people are tempted, so it's good to know I'm normal. Thank You, God, that You have promised to help me be strong—and will show me a way out! Thank You for being greater than any temptation I may face. Amen.

The temptations in your life are no different from what others experience. And God is faithful. He will not allow the temptation to be more than you can stand. When you are tempted, he will show you a way out so that you can endure.
1 CORINTHIANS 10:13 NLT

FORGIVING MYSELF

Dear God, I get so frustrated with myself sometimes when I mess up. I know that I can never do things perfectly, but I still have that desire in my heart. When I see how far I really am from perfect, it sometimes makes me feel hopeless, like there's no point in even trying to be good. When I start thinking this way, help me to remember that You didn't create me to be perfect and that what I do has no impact on how much You love me. There is nothing that I could do to earn Your love, and I thank You for that gift. Amen.

If you kept record of our sins, no one could last long. But you forgive us, and so we will worship you.
PSALM 130:3–4 CEV

JUST BEIN' ME

Lord, why is it so hard not to want to be someone else? Everywhere I look there is someone with "more" than what I have. The problem is, the more I notice what others have, the less I can see the blessings You have given *me*. I know there are many people with less than what I am complaining about having!

Father God, please help me to see the positive, to enjoy the ordinary and appreciate what I do have, and to not complain about what I don't have in my life. If I am focusing on others instead of You, my view becomes blurred.

Teach me to recognize all You have given me and help me to become all You created me to be. Amen.

Let us not become conceited, or provoke one another, or be jealous of one another.
GALATIANS 5:26 NLT

MY SELFISHNESS

Lord, I can be very selfish in every area of my life. I am selfish with my time, my possessions, my friends, and a lot of other things. I don't want to constantly think only of myself; I want to be unselfish and serve those around me in any way that I can. Make my heart sensitive to the needs of those around me, and make me alert to my own selfishness, especially when it comes to helping others. You have said that the greatest commandments are to love You and to love my neighbor as myself; help me to do both of those things in my daily life. Amen.

Do nothing out of selfish ambition or vain conceit.
Rather, in humility value others above yourselves,
not looking to your own interests but each
of you to the interests of the others.
PHILIPPIANS 2:3–4 NIV

LONELINESS

I know You have promised to never leave me, God—but sometimes I just need a real person to be there for me. All the difficulties of life can pile up until I am totally overwhelmed, and even in the midst of family and friends I feel alone. Like no one can really understand what I am going through, even like no one cares. While my head may tell me that's not true, that's still the way I *feel*.

In Philippians 4:19, Your word tells me that You will supply everything I need.

There *are* people in my life who love me and care about me. You have placed them there because You care for me most of all. When loneliness or circumstances overwhelm me, remind me of Your love for me. Amen.

꙳

When I am overwhelmed,
you alone know the way I should turn.
PSALM 142:3 NLT

THOSE WHO WAIT

Forgive me for my impatience, Lord. Sometimes I make a request and wonder if You've even heard me when I don't receive an answer right away. And sometimes I think You've forgotten me or stopped listening to my prayers altogether. But I know that isn't true. Sometimes You say "wait," just like I have to wait for other things in life.

Please help me as I wait. I know I can pray in faith and You *will* answer. It just might not be as fast as I'd like—but I do trust that Your timing will *always* be perfect. Amen.

We do not want you to become lazy,
but to imitate those who through faith and
patience inherit what has been promised.
HEBREWS 6:12 NIV

ME AND MY BIG MOUTH!

Oh my big mouth! Lord, sometimes it gets me in trouble. I don't mean to spout off, but sometimes I feel like a teakettle, overflowing with hot water and covering the whole room! I get upset, and things just come racing out of my lips before I can even think them through. Before long, I've "burned" all sorts of people with my ugly words.

Forgive me for this, Lord, and help me change. Make my words gentle. I know that You want me to guard my tongue. Please help me with this! I need to know how to react when I'm faced with a situation that's tough. I don't want to spout off like that teakettle. I want to react calmly. Amen.

∽

*To speak evil of no one, to avoid quarreling,
to be gentle, and to show perfect
courtesy toward all people.*
TITUS 3:2 ESV

MY LIFE IS YOURS

Father, I'm sorry for the times I have tried to take things into my own hands and do things on my own. That never seems to work out for the best. I know the safest place for me to be is in Your care because You see the "big picture" of my life and know what's best for me.

Lord Jesus, I want You to have complete control. Help me to recognize the times I try to take over so that I can ask for Your forgiveness and follow Your way. Amen.

Therefore, I urge you, brothers and sisters, in view of God's mercy, to offer your bodies as a living sacrifice, holy and pleasing to God—this is your true and proper worship.
ROMANS 12:1 NIV

GOD'S DELIGHT

You are with me. You are a mighty Savior. You take great delight in me. You will calm me with Your love. You even rejoice over me with singing!

Help me to remember these words in times of fear and stress, heavenly Father. I will need these words to quiet my heart for the rest of my life. You've told me that I'll have trouble in this broken world, but You've also told me to take heart because You have overcome it (John 16:33)! Thank You for this amazing reminder. Amen.

"For the LORD your God is living among you. He is a mighty savior. He will take delight in you with gladness. With his love, he will calm all your fears. He will rejoice over you with joyful songs."
ZEPHANIAH 3:17 NLT

THE TRUTH!

Father, forgive me when I lie. Sometimes when I'm put on the spot, it seems easier to lie than to tell the truth. Immediately, I know I've sinned, and I regret it. I realize that if I continue to lie, I will become more likely to repeat those lies; eventually, lying will become a sinful habit. And lies only lead to trouble!

Please help me when I'm tempted to lie—no matter how hard it might be to tell the truth. Even in those moments when I'm afraid of the consequences, remind me to do what's right. Amen.

So stop telling lies. Let us tell our neighbors the truth, for we are all parts of the same body.
EPHESIANS 4:25 NLT

CAN'T DECIDE?

Making decisions is hard, but the truth is that I don't need to worry about those things or make any decisions on my own. You, my God, greet me each morning with Your love. If I take a few minutes in the morning to pray, You help me through whatever I might have to face and any decisions I need to make.

Help me today, Father. Let Your love guide my path in whatever decisions I face. Show me the way when I'm clueless. I depend on You to help me make the right decisions. Amen.

Let me hear of your unfailing love each morning, for I am trusting you. Show me where to walk, for I give myself to you.
Psalm 143:8 NLT

A WORK IN PROGRESS

Father, just like a sculptor uses his skilled hands to transform a lump of clay into something extraordinary, You are steadily molding me into the woman I will one day become. And even then, I will still be imperfect. You will always be teaching me and perfecting me—until Jesus comes back. Thank You that it is okay to be imperfect. You have begun something great in me, and I am a wonderful work in progress. I love You, Lord. Amen.

And I am certain that God, who began the good work within you, will continue his work until it is finally finished on the day when Christ Jesus returns.

PHILIPPIANS 1:6 NLT

COMFORT FROM GOD

Heavenly Father, thank You for being there for me. Help me to feel Your presence in my heart, even if I can't see You with my eyes. I want to be comforted by Your scripture and by being able to talk to You; remind me of these things when I'm feeling lonely or depressed. I know that all comfort and all love comes from You. I just forget that sometimes. Help me to always remember Your love and Your comfort that is in my heart. Thank You for providing people who love me and can hug me and listen to me and speak words of wisdom into my life. Amen.

Show me a sign of your goodness. When my enemies look, they will be ashamed. You, LORD, have helped me and comforted me.
PSALM 86:17 NCV

LOVING MY ENEMIES

I don't know if I have many enemies, Lord, but I do know there are a lot of people who don't like the fact that I'm a Christian. They don't believe in You, and they're looking for any chance they can get to argue Your existence and make me feel stupid for believing.

Help me to love them anyway. Let them see little glimpses of Your power and love through me. Help me to be strong in You and in Your mighty power. Use me to bring light and love into the darkness. Amen.

"Love your enemies! Do good to them. Lend to them without expecting to be repaid. Then your reward from heaven will be very great, and you will truly be acting as children of the Most High, for he is kind to those who are unthankful and wicked."
LUKE 6:35 NLT

DON'T JUDGE ME

Lord, I hate when people decide things about me that aren't true. They make a "judgment" about my clothes, where I live, the color of my hair or skin, the way I talk or look.

But if I'm honest, I would have to say I sometimes do the same thing. If I'm not careful, I can make judgments about others based on what I believe to be true, but it's possible to not have the full story or to have an opinion without all the facts. I really don't want to do that!

Help me to see people for who they really are and treat them as I want to be treated. Amen.

"Don't judge others, and you will not be judged. Don't accuse others of being guilty, and you will not be accused of being guilty. Forgive, and you will be forgiven."
Luke 6:37 NCV

DELIGHT IN HIM

There are so many things I want, Lord. New clothes, gadgets, stuff for my room. . . . I want things for my life too. I want to be popular. I want to make good grades. I want to be the best at the things I love to do. Sometimes I want those things so much it hurts.

But You said I'm supposed to want You more than I want anything else. I'm supposed to delight in You. I know You love me, and that makes me smile. But I know I could think about You more and spend more time doing things that make You happy. Help me, today and every day, to delight in You. Amen.

Take delight in the LORD, and he will give you the desires of your heart.
PSALM 37:4 NIV

THANKFUL FOR MY FAMILY

Dear Lord, thank You for parents who love me and guide me and siblings who play with me and encourage me. Thank You for extended family like grandparents, cousins, aunts, and uncles. You have provided me with so many people who love me and care about me. I realize there are kids out there who aren't as blessed in this area as I am. I pray that You would be their family and their support, that they would feel You in their lives. Help me to be aware of people like that in my life and to reach out and love them and be their family. And thank You for friends who feel like family and welcome me into their homes with loving arms. Amen.

"Respect your father and mother. And love others as much as you love yourself."
MATTHEW 19:19 CEV

STUDY HELP

I sometimes wonder if all the studying is worth it, Jesus. But I know You want me to do my best in everything I do, which includes my schoolwork. Help me to have a better attitude about it and want to do a good job.

I ask for Your help in getting through these classes. Help me, please, to study what I need to, and for the length of time that I should. Please teach me how to avoid distractions so that I can reach my goals and finish well. . .so I can even have some fun time when the work is done. Amen.

Do your best to present yourself to God as one approved, a worker who has no need to be ashamed, rightly handling the word of truth.
2 TIMOTHY 2:15 ESV

THE UPS AND DOWNS
OF FRIENDSHIP

Thank You for my many friends, heavenly Father. Some friends have let me down (and more will!). Help me to be quick to forgive them when that happens. I pray that I won't let others down, but if I do, that I will be quick to ask for forgiveness and make the relationship right again.

I ask for wisdom in choosing my friends. I ask that You guide me to the ones who will be a good influence and will encourage me in my walk with You. Thank You for being the most perfect friend anyone could ever have. Amen.

Some friends don't help, but a true friend is closer than your own family.
PROVERBS 18:24 CEV

THE PRESENT MOMENT

Sometimes, Father, I want to be so grown-up. Then at other times, I'm so glad I'm not yet an adult. Older people seem to have so many responsibilities—ones I'm definitely not ready for.

Help me to be happy in the present moment, Lord. To live for today and not worry about tomorrow. Remind me that every day with You is a good day.

Give me the strength to be patient and the wisdom to know what is good for me at whatever age I am. Thank You, Lord, for being with me every stage of my life, gently leading me, tenderly supporting me, and blessing me day after day. Amen.

This is the day the Lord has made;
We will rejoice and be glad in it.
PSALM 118:24 NKJV

HAPPY IN HOPING

Lord, life can really hurt! But I'm glad I know about You and the purpose my relationship with You brings to my life. No matter how bad things get, I know there is always hope because You promised You'd never leave me and that someday I'll live with You.

Sometimes I overhear others talking about the bad things happening in their lives, and they seem to have no hope at all. What a terrible feeling that must be! Help me to share with them the solid hope I have because of You and the strength that gives me to get up each morning and know I can make it with Your help. I love You, Jesus! Amen.

Blessed are those whose help is the God of Jacob, whose hope is in the Lord their God.
PSALM 146:5 NIV

LET SOMEBODY ELSE

I'm good at a lot of things, Lord. I have many things I like to do, many things I do well. The problem is, not everyone knows about all the things I'm good at. Sometimes other people get recognized for things, and I get ignored. That's not fun.

Help me to remember that no matter how hard it is to feel passed over and ignored, it's usually best to stay quiet about my own strengths. I should do my best in everything and let others figure out what I'm good at. Praise always feels better when it comes from someone else and not from my own mouth.

Remind me of that today, Lord. Amen.

Let someone else praise you, and not your own mouth; an outsider, and not your own lips.
PROVERBS 27:2 NIV

GUILTY FEELINGS

Dear God, I feel guilty today. I know that You are a God of mercy and forgiveness, so I'm coming to You right now and asking You to make me clean. I've sinned, and I know it. Please forgive me and restore me in Your sight, and let me be wiser and on my guard against temptation.

I'm glad that Jesus died for my sins and that You are ready to forgive when I ask. Thank You for loving me always. In Jesus' name, amen.

If we confess our sins, He is faithful and just to forgive us our sins and to cleanse us from all unrighteousness.
1 JOHN 1:9 NKJV

WHAT REALLY MATTERS

Lord, sometimes I feel so different from other kids because I go to church and try to follow You. Yet deep in my heart, I know that You are real and that I am on the right path and that's what matters.

Please show me how I can show Your love to everyone I meet, how I can follow Your commandment to love You with all my heart, soul, and mind, and to love others as I love myself. Give me the peace that comes from following You. And help me to encourage others as You encourage me. In Jesus' name I pray, amen.

Some people have gotten out of the habit of meeting for worship, but we must not do that. We should keep on encouraging each other, especially since you know that the day of the Lord's coming is getting closer.
Hebrews 10:25 cev

FORGIVE THEM?

You really expect me to *forgive* them, Jesus? After what they did to me? I can usually let a lot of things go but not this time. This time it hurts too much.

Jesus, I know You understand what this is like. Your friend took a bribe to turn You in when You hadn't done anything wrong. And You were killed in such a cruel way. But some of Your last words were ones of forgiveness. How was that possible?

And Jesus, I have hurt You with my sin, but You keep forgiving *me* anyway. Please give me the strength to be like You. Amen.

Be kind to one another, tenderhearted, forgiving one another, as God in Christ forgave you.
EPHESIANS 4:32 ESV

AMAZING LOVE

It's so hard for me to wrap my head around the idea that You, Father—a big God, the Creator of the universe—could love and care for me *even when I mess up!*

Thank You, Father, for Your constant, unchanging love. Thank You for creating me and giving me new life through Your Son, Jesus. I pray that I will return that love through a life that brings You glory and honor. Amen.

When I look at the night sky and see the work of your fingers—the moon and the stars you set in place—what are mere mortals that you should think about them, human beings that you should care for them?
PSALM 8:3–4 NLT

SELF-DISCIPLINE

Lord, I have to admit, it's not always easy to do everything I'm told. When my parents give me instructions, I should follow them, but sometimes I slack off. I get busy doing other things and forget. Unless they remind me, I don't always get things done. Then my parents discipline me. Embarrassing!

Please teach me how to be self-disciplined, Lord. Can You remind me to take care of things and show me how to be responsible? I want to grow up to be the very best me I can possibly be! With Your help, I know I can do it! Amen.

For the Spirit God gave us does not make us timid, but gives us power, love and self-discipline.
2 TIMOTHY 1:7 NIV

WHEN I FEEL INSECURE

Heavenly Father, I feel so insecure sometimes. I feel insecure about what others think of me, how I look or dress, and whether or not anyone actually likes me. I don't want to feel this way, and I don't always know what to do when this happens. Whenever I'm feeling insecure, help me to remember to turn to You and look to You for the security that I need. Nothing else will bring lasting security, no matter how hard I try or whom I listen to—true peace of mind will come from only You. Thank You for Your constant love and security. Amen.

Only God can save me, and I calmly wait for him. God alone is the mighty rock that keeps me safe and the fortress where I am secure.
PSALM 62:1–2 CEV

HUMILITY

Lord, help me to remember that none of my goals can be met on my own. I need Your help. And when I am in leadership roles or win an award of any kind, I want to always remember to give You the glory. I will serve as a leader at my school or church or in any situation You see fit. But even if I rise to the top, let me always remember You are above me. I am Your humble servant. Use me and give me opportunities to build others up. I don't want to be jealous if someone outshines me. Help me to always choose humility. Amen.

Whoever is the greatest should be the servant of the others. If you put yourself above others, you will be put down. But if you humble yourself, you will be honored.
MATTHEW 23:11–12 CEV

WORDS CAN HURT YOU

"Sticks and stones may break my bones, but words can never hurt me." Not true! Words have the power to cause great pain. They can slice and wound so deep that healing from them may seem impossible. I've seen it happen—relationships that are never the same after careless words are spoken.

God, please help me to guard my mouth so that I never hurt others as I have been hurt by thoughtless words. Help me to be kind to others, and when they are unkind to me, help me to forgive them. Help me to respond to those around me in a way that is honoring to them—and to You. Amen.

Just as damaging as a madman shooting a deadly weapon is someone who lies to a friend and then says, "I was only joking."
PROVERBS 26:18–19 NLT

WHY WORRY? PRAY!

Father, each day gives me something new to worry about! Yet You tell Your children not to worry and to pray instead. I need help with that, Lord. My first reaction is to fret rather than pray. I know You care about me and the things I care about. So remind me of that when my own thoughts cause me such unrest and conflict.

Father, I give You all of my worries right now and ask that You help me to sort through them. Please give me the answers I need and the peace that comes with surrendering my problems and concerns to You. Amen.

Don't worry about anything; instead, pray about everything. Tell God what you need, and thank him for all he has done. Then you will experience God's peace.
PHILIPPIANS 4:6–7 NLT

A MEASURE OF LOVE

Heavenly Father, help me not to condemn and judge other people when I have no right to do that. I'm not You. But when a friend of mine is choosing sin over Your plan, help me to be able to talk to her out of love and friendship instead of acting like I know it all and that I have everything figured out. Give me wisdom to confront the friends that I feel You nudging me to talk to. But help me always to do it in love—with a clean heart before You. Amen.

*"For in the same way you judge others,
you will be judged, and with the measure
you use, it will be measured to you."*
MATTHEW 7:2 NIV

LIVING WITHOUT REGRETS

Heavenly Father, I'm struggling with guilt from a bad choice. It feels like it's strapped to my back and I'll need to carry it every day for the rest of my life. I feel like I need to keep saying I'm sorry. Or maybe I need to do a lot of good things to make up for it.

No, Your Word tells me that if I say I'm sorry for my sin, You will take it away. But not only that, You choose to forget about it!

Lord Jesus, I ask for Your forgiveness for what I've done. Help me to trust that You forgive me and won't hold my sin against me. Thank You, Father! In Jesus' name, amen.

"For I will forgive their wickedness and will remember their sins no more."
HEBREWS 8:12 NIV

WHAT'S HAPPENING TOMORROW?

Sometimes I wish I could see into the future, Lord! I wish I knew what I will be when I'm all grown up. One day I'll know the answer to that question, but in the meantime, please help me with all of the changes I'm going through—in my body, my mind, and my heart. Seems like every day I'm changing a little more.

Everyone goes through changes, so I know I'm not the only one. And I'm sure everyone gets a little scared about the future. Remind me that You've got this, Lord! You will direct my path and will give me wisdom as I go through changes, large or small! Amen.

Trust in the LORD with all your heart
and lean not on your own understanding;
in all your ways submit to him,
and he will make your paths straight.
PROVERBS 3:5–6 NIV

POPULARITY

God, I really want people to like me and to want to be around me. When I'm in a situation where I feel pressure to do things because they are "cool," help me to stop and think about what I'm doing and not give in to the pressure of my peers. Help me to stand up for what I believe and show others that I believe in You and want to glorify You with my words and actions. The main goal in my life shouldn't be popularity, and sometimes I forget that. Please help me to remember, and be patient with me when I mess up. Amen.

So with God and Christ as witnesses, I command you to preach God's message. Do it willingly, even if it isn't the popular thing to do.
2 TIMOTHY 4:1–2 CEV

QUIET TIME

Dear God, help me to be faithful in spending time with You regularly, building my relationship with You, and not just when I need Your help. When things are going well in my life, I tend to forget that You want my company and want me to talk to You. But the second that things get hard, You are the first person I want to talk to and share my problems with. Help me to remember that You are more than just a "fixer" and that I should talk to You about all the good things in my life, not just the bad. Amen.

I thirst for the living God.
When can I go to meet with him?
PSALM 42:2 NCV

A PURPOSE AND A PLAN

God, when disappointment comes, I find myself getting grouchy and pouting. But behaving that way doesn't make me feel any better. In fact, it makes me feel worse.

Your Word says that You are working out for my good everything that happens in my life. You have a plan and purpose for me. So help me to just shrug off disappointment when things don't go my way. Help me to look on the bright side, seeing Your hand in my life, knowing that You know and want what's best for me—You have a better way. Amen.

And we know that God causes everything to work together for the good of those who love God and are called according to his purpose for them.
ROMANS 8:28 NLT

COPYCAT

Lord, I look around at school and at the mall and I see everyone trying to fit in. I get really confused about this kind of stuff because I want to fit in too. But I want to please You even more. Help me not to care so much about what other people think. Amen.

And so, dear brothers and sisters, I plead with you to give your bodies to God because of all he has done for you. Let them be a living and holy sacrifice—the kind he will find acceptable. This is truly the way to worship him. Don't copy the behavior and customs of this world, but let God transform you into a new person by changing the way you think. Then you will learn to know God's will for you, which is good and pleasing and perfect.
ROMANS 12:1–2 NLT

TELL THE TRUTH

Lord, I don't want to be left in the dark about things. I would much rather someone come to me and tell me what is going on, even if it is painful, so I think that is the best way for me to behave too. I think You honor truth, Lord. There's a verse in the Bible that talks about "speaking the truth in love" (Ephesians 4:15 NKJV). I think that means that we can be truthful, but at the same time we can be kind to others. It means speaking *truth*, not repeating gossip or our own and others' opinions. I think it means to speak Your truth found in Your Word.

God, help me to lovingly speak truth to others. Amen.

Gentle words are a tree of life;
a deceitful tongue crushes the spirit.
PROVERBS 15:4 NLT

THE RUMOR MILL

Sometimes I get caught up in gossip, Lord, and I end up feeling really bad in the end. Gossip is like a forest fire! It spreads and spreads and hurts a lot of people in the process. Can You help me to put out the forest fire instead of spreading it? When someone tells me some "juicy gossip," please close my mouth! Don't let me spread it to anyone else. Instead, remind me to pray for the person who's being gossiped about and to keep my heart pure. I want to be known as someone who brings people together, not someone who divides friends by gossiping. Amen.

Whoever covers an offense seeks love, but he who repeats a matter separates close friends.
PROVERBS 17:9 ESV

PRIDE

Dear Lord, help me to be humble. When I take pride in my grades or my success in sports or my appearance, I need to remember that You are the one who has given me these abilities and that I should be humble and thankful for what You have given. I know there is nothing wrong with being confident in the gifts that You have given me, but I don't want to brag and base my self-worth in things that I do. When I'm tempted to brag or take too much pride in something, please humble my spirit and remind me that everything I have is a blessing that comes from You. Amen.

*Too much pride can put you to shame.
It's wiser to be humble.*
PROVERBS 11:2 CEV

TOUGH STUFF!

Lord, sometimes I think I don't have enough energy to get everything done. Schoolwork. After-school activities. Family stuff. Church obligations. I feel like I'm in over my head sometimes. How can I possibly get everything done and still get a good night's sleep?

Show me what's important to do, Father. I don't want to do stuff just to stay busy. I want the "stuff" I do to be important to You. So, if there's anything in my life I'm not supposed to be doing, show me. Help me to create a schedule that works for me and my family, one that leaves me plenty of time to pray and spend time in Your Word. Amen.

*From the ends of the earth, I cry to you
for help when my heart is overwhelmed.
Lead me to the towering rock of safety.*
PSALM 61:2 NLT

I'M LISTENING TO YOU!

Lord, I want to be better at listening to You. No, it may not be an audible voice, but You can speak in so many ways. You can point out sins that I've forgotten about. You can bring someone to mind whom I need to pray for, or even someone I need to share with who doesn't know You yet.

Please, Jesus, help me to be quiet and listen for Your voice. I want to hear what You have to say to me. Amen.

*If you call out for insight and raise your voice
for understanding, if you seek it like silver
and search for it as for hidden treasures,
then you will understand the fear of the
LORD and find the knowledge of God.*
PROVERBS 2:3–5 ESV

LOVE AND RESPECT

God, I hear that I should fear You. I want to better understand what that means. Why should I fear You if You're good and kind? I guess it's like having a healthy fear of my parents. I know they love me, but if I do something they've told me not to they will punish me because they want me to learn the best way to live.

I love You, Lord. I also understand that You are God, and if I go against Your ways, You will discipline me because You love me and You want the best for me. Thank You for loving me that much. Help me to always have the right kind of respect for You. Amen.

"These are the ones I look on with favor:
those who are humble and contrite in spirit,
and who tremble at my word."
ISAIAH 66:2 NIV

DEPENDING ON GOD

Lord, so often I just jump into things without talking them over with You. I want to do better about that. I want us to become so close that I wouldn't think of making plans without You. Can we be a team?

As I get older, I will have even more decisions to make, such as where to go to school or what career to pursue. I will have choices regarding marriage and children, where to live, and all sorts of things. While I am young, I want to get into the habit of walking with You. I commit my ways to You, Lord. Please bless me and allow my plans to succeed. I will give You all the glory. Amen.

Depend on the LORD in whatever you do,
and your plans will succeed.
PROVERBS 16:3 NCV

BLESSED ALL OVER AGAIN

Open my eyes, Lord, to everything around me. Help me to realize that in a world where so many people have so little, I have so very much.

Your Word tells me that it is so much more wonderful to give than to receive. Create in me a grateful spirit and a heart that loves to share. Show me what I might give away to bless the lives of others. When I make it all about pleasing You—by giving from the bottom of my heart—I find myself blessed all over again! Amen.

"All must give as they are able, according to the blessings given to them by the LORD your God."
DEUTERONOMY 16:17 NLT

TRUST IN THE LORD

God, there have been times when I have trusted someone and he or she has really let me down. It hurts! After a while, it causes me not to trust anyone or anything. I don't want to be rejected again or disappointed when someone doesn't remain true.

Help me to realize that it will always be a tricky balance to determine which people in my life to trust. But I can always trust You. You will never leave me or lead me down a wrong path. You promise to direct me and to make Your plans clear to me as I journey through life. Amen.

Those who know the LORD trust him, because he will not leave those who come to him.
PSALM 9:10 NCV

A SERVANT'S HEART

Dear Lord, as someone who believes in You and what You teach, I am called to a life of serving others and putting them before myself. But because we were all created differently, You have given us different ways of serving each other. Help me to use the gifts and abilities that You have given me in a unique way to serve those around me. Thank You for the gifts and abilities that You have given me. Help me not to compare them to anyone else's and to be thankful in everything. Please show me how to serve You, be a good example, and have a servant's heart for my friends, family, and acquaintances. Amen.

*The Spirit has given each of us
a special way of serving others.*
1 CORINTHIANS 12:7 CEV

GOD UNDERSTANDS

Lord, I'm so frustrated. No one understands me. I try to believe that You understand me. Do You really get how hard this life can be? I guess You do. You came down here from heaven. The Bible says there are no tears and no pain there. I'm amazed that You left that glorious place to come to earth. You wanted people like me to know that You walked where we walk.

Jesus, when no one else understands me, remind me that You do. Even though You are God, You lived here as a child and grew into a man. You experienced this life. You get it. Thanks, Jesus. Amen.

He had to be one of us, so that he could serve God as our merciful and faithful high priest and sacrifice himself for the forgiveness of our sins.
HEBREWS 2:17 CEV

GIVE ME COURAGE, PLEASE

Heavenly Father, I want to be courageous. Sometimes I face problems that seem too tough to handle. I've read about people of courage in the Bible like David and Ruth and Daniel and Esther and Mary and Paul and so many more.

I need the kind of courage and confidence they had too. I don't want to be weak and cowardly and ashamed of You and Your Word. I want to be bold in my witness for You; I want to live courageously. I ask this in Your name. Amen.

*"Be strong and of good courage, do not
fear nor be afraid of them; for the LORD your
God, He is the One who goes with you.
He will not leave you nor forsake you."*
DEUTERONOMY 31:6 NKJV

SECOND PLACE

Lord, sometimes I feel second best. Thank You for not having favorites. I can run to You and know that You always have time for me and love me unconditionally because all of Your children are number one to You. Help me to continue doing my best, knowing it's for You. . .and that You're the only one who really matters. I don't want to keep trying to do better and better, only to fail again. But in Your eyes, I'm not a failure!

On days when I get discouraged, I ask that You comfort me in the way that only a best friend can. Thank You, Lord. Amen.

"Look at the birds of the air: they neither sow nor reap nor gather into barns, and yet your heavenly Father feeds them. Are you not of more value than they?"
MATTHEW 6:26 ESV

LOTS TO LEARN

Dear Father, thank You for teachers. Yes, I know sometimes I complain about the homework they assign and the tests they give, but I want to say thank You anyway. Forgive me for the times I've been disrespectful in my attitude and words about my teachers.

Thank You that I live in a country where education is available to everyone. Thank You for the teachers who get up every morning and come to class and answer my questions and grade my papers. Help me to show them that I appreciate them. Amen.

❧

Listen to advice and accept discipline, and at the end you will be counted among the wise.
PROVERBS 19:20 NIV

AS PURE AS SNOW

Lord, I know the Bible says You want us to be pure, not just in our hearts, but in our outward appearance—the way we dress ourselves. Help me not to fall into the trap of wanting to dress like my friends or talk like my friends if it's not pleasing to You. What matters most is that people know I'm Yours!

Remind me every day, Lord, that staying in Your Word is the very best way to keep my heart innocent and clean. May I always shine like the glistening white snow for You! Amen.

How can a young person stay on the path of purity? By living according to your word.
Psalm 119:9 niv

SPEAK UP!

Lord, I love You with all my heart. But sometimes it's hard to talk about You in front of my friends. They don't all feel the same about You, and if I talk about You too much, they might think I'm weird.

It's not that I'm ashamed of You, Lord. I just don't always know how to bring You into the conversation. I want my friends to know about You. I want them to know how cool and awesome and amazing You are. I want them to know how much You love them.

Help me to know how to tell others about You, Lord. Help me to know when to speak and when to stay quiet, showing Your love through my actions. Give me courage. Amen.

"I tell you," he replied, "if they keep quiet, the stones will cry out."
LUKE 19:40 NIV

WAiT!

Some days it feels like everything is moving so slowly. I should be patient, Lord, but that's so much easier to say than do. Maybe I'm moving too fast. And I suppose I'm being a little bit selfish too.

Please help me to learn to slow down, Jesus. Let me take a breath and learn how to wait. A lot of good things take time: flowers growing, good friendships, even a cake baking. None of that can be hurried. Help me to be patient like You want me to be. Amen.

See how the farmer waits for the precious fruit of the earth, being patient about it, until it receives the early and the late rains. You also, be patient.
JAMES 5:7–8 ESV

GRANDPARENTS ARE GREAT

Dear God, I'm so thankful to have grandparents who love me and teach me and are there for me through anything.

My grandparents still show off my picture to strangers and sometimes embarrass me with their hugs, but they're really cool anyway, and I know they want the best for me. When I've had a hard day at school, they understand and let me talk it out. When I visit them, they buy special food for me and let me stay up late.

So I'm saying a prayer of thanks for my grandparents and also praying for them. Please take care of them and keep them healthy and let me have them in my life for a long time. Help me to be a good granddaughter. I ask this in Jesus' name, amen.

Grandchildren are the crowning glory of the aged.
PROVERBS 17:6 NLT

GETTING MY WAY

Oh boy, am I stubborn sometimes, Lord! I want to stomp my foot when I don't get my own way, to demand that people give me what I want. And if they don't give it to me, sometimes my attitude really stinks. Oh help! I need You to remind me every day that what really matters isn't getting my own way; it's humbling myself and becoming more like You. Can You help me with this?

Jesus didn't demand His own way. He prayed and asked His Father (You!) what to do. . .then He did it. No arguments. No foot stomping. He listened and then obeyed. I want to be like Jesus, Father! Amen.

Pride goes before destruction,
a haughty spirit before a fall.
PROVERBS 16:18 NIV

WHAT DO I DO NOW?

God, help me to recognize Your way for me, to do what will please You, not others. Happiness is temporary. Joy—which comes from You—lasts forever. Help me to make wise decisions in my life. Wisdom from Your Word brings success. It will bring more than I can hope for if I follow it instead of choosing my own path.

Wisdom is using good judgment. It is more than doing what others around me are doing or telling me I should do. It goes beyond just "following the crowd." Help me to make good decisions, Lord—decisions that will please You. Amen.

For wisdom is far more valuable than rubies.
Nothing you desire can compare with it.
PROVERBS 8:11 NLT

ENVY

God, I struggle with envy a lot. Whenever my friends get the latest phone or new clothes, I want the same things and it makes me miserable. And whenever I am jealous of my friends, it makes me act unkindly toward them, and I know that isn't right. Please help me to be happy for them when good things come their way. I would want them to be happy for me if our roles were reversed, and I don't want to be jealous—it's an ugly attitude. Help me to be content with the things that I do have and to be thankful for having so much when so many people in the world have so little. Amen.

I realized the reason people work hard and try to succeed: They are jealous of each other. This, too, is useless, like chasing the wind.
ECCLESIASTES 4:4 NCV

SURPRISES AND WONDERS

Lord, many of my friends seem to be playing follow-the-leader. Everyone does what everyone else is doing—whether it's wrong or right. But *You* are the true leader. You are the hero that will never fall. So I want to follow and imitate You—not the latest movie star, sports figure, or even the most popular kid in school.

Lord, instead of worshipping the things and people of this world, I want to worship You—and You alone. If I take a course that seems different to others, I'm okay with that, for I know You will always be with me. Thank You for leading me *Your* way. Amen.

Do not conform to the pattern of this world, but be transformed by the renewing of your mind. Then you will be able to test and approve what God's will is.
ROMANS 12:2 NIV

WHAT ABOUT ME?

Heavenly Father, Your Word reminds us that we should keep on doing good. You promise to reward us for all our effort (Galatians 6:9). Because of Your promise, Father, I'm asking that You help me to keep my focus on others instead of myself. I know You *always* see what I do to make a difference in the world, even when others don't see or don't care. And if You see, then that's enough for me! When others overlook or forget my kindness, it is so wonderful to know that You never will!

Please help me to keep up the good work, God. And I'll be looking to see what good things You have in store for me. Amen.

Let us not become weary in doing good, for at the proper time we will reap a harvest if we do not give up.
GALATIANS 6:9 NIV

COLLECTING THINGS

Dear Lord, thank You for all the things that You have given me. I don't want to base my self-worth on the things that I have, but it's so easy sometimes to make myself feel better with a new outfit or new technology. Remind me that the things I possess don't have any lasting value and will not bring me closer to You. My purpose in life shouldn't be to collect the biggest and the best things the world has to offer; it should be to glorify You in everything I say and do. Thank You for providing for me emotionally and spiritually as well as physically. Amen.

Then he said to them, "Watch out! Be on your guard against all kinds of greed; life does not consist in an abundance of possessions."
LUKE 12:15 NIV

A TRUE FRIEND

Lord, teach me to make good compromises with my friends, sometimes doing what they want to do rather than always trying to get my own way. Make me the type of friend who respects others, not someone who is two-faced, acting one way in my friend's presence and then talking bad about her behind her back. I don't like it when someone does that to me, so I never want to hurt someone that way.

God, You have blessed me with some good friends. Help me to treat them kindly even when we disagree. And where there is a need in my life for a friend, lead me to one that will be a true friend to me. I need wisdom as I choose godly friends. Amen.

And Jonathan made a covenant with David because he loved him as himself.
1 SAMUEL 18:3 NIV

WHAT'S IMPORTANT

Even though I can't see You, God, I know that You are there. I know You are good and that You love me beyond what I can imagine. I want to know You better. Your Word tells me who You are, and the truth found there helps me to understand what You have to say about Yourself. I know there are a lot of opinions about who You are, and there are many people who can help me learn, but I need to go to the Source—You.

There is so much I don't know and can't understand about You, God! But thank You for giving us the Bible to read. Give me more understanding of who You are. Amen.

"Yes, a person is a fool to store up earthly wealth but not have a rich relationship with God."
Luke 12:21 NLT

WHAT JOY!

Lord, I want my heart to be filled with joy. When people look at me, I want them to say, "Wow! That girl is always smiling! She seems so full of joy and life!" I don't want a fake smile. I want a real one!

I know that real joy comes from spending time with You, Father. Remind me of that when I start to feel down, okay? Don't let me slip too far away from You. Keep my heart close to Yours so that Your joy will fill me up, bubbling inside of me until it spills over onto everything I see each day. What fun that will be, to live a joyous life! Amen.

Rejoice in the Lord always;
I will say it again: Rejoice!
PHILIPPIANS 4:4 NIV

A TEMPLE

Lord, I want to take better care of my body, not just to look pretty but to be healthy and honor the body that You have created and given me. So whenever I'm tempted to eat more than I'm hungry for, I need to remember that probably isn't the best. And it's so hard for me to get all the rest I need sometimes. So please help me to have self-control when it comes to taking care of my body and making sure that I am treating it with the respect it deserves. Amen.

You surely know that your body is a temple where the Holy Spirit lives. The Spirit is in you and is a gift from God. You are no longer your own. God paid a great price for you. So use your body to honor God.
1 CORINTHIANS 6:19–20 CEV

FUTURE FRIENDS

Sometimes I fight with them and sometimes I stick up for them, but Lord, my siblings are here to stay. We're part of the same family, yet we're very different. Maybe one of the reasons You put me into a family is so I would learn to share and think about somebody besides me. Even though I don't get along with them all the time, I do love my siblings, and I want us to have a good relationship someday. Help me to remember to think before I speak and to respect their space and their stuff. Show me how to be kind even when I don't feel like it. Amen.

A friend is always loyal, and a brother is born to help in time of need.
PROVERBS 17:17 NLT

LIKE AN EAGLE

Lord, sometimes I get frustrated and tired and want to give up. I start thinking that I can't do anything right, that I've let down my parents, teachers, and friends. But then I remember as long as I look to and hope in You, I will get strong again—and perhaps get the grade, make the team, or find an awesome way to lend a helping hand to others.

Give me the strength to keep trying. Give me the energy to soar like an eagle, rising up to meet Your love and power. Amen.

Even youths grow tired and weary, and. . . stumble and fall; but those who hope in the LORD will renew their strength. They will soar on wings like eagles; they will run and not grow weary, they will walk and not be faint.
ISAIAH 40:30–31 NIV

THE ROUGH PLACES

Lord, You never promised life would be fair. Actually, it seems like the more hard stuff we go through, the more we have to depend on You to help us deal with it. And that's good.

I always want to pray for things to go smoothly in my life, Lord. But I wonder if it's not the rough places that help smooth out my character. I'm not going to ask You to make my life hard. That would be crazy. But I will pray that You use the difficult things in my life to make me more like You. Amen.

"I have told you all this so that you may have peace in me. Here on earth you will have many trials and sorrows. But take heart, because I have overcome the world."
JOHN 16:33 NLT

LOVELY PETALS

Lord, sometimes I think my relationship with You is like a flower opening up on a sunny day. When I gave You my heart, You planted my little seed of faith, and now it's growing, growing, growing! Every day another petal opens up as I change and grow to become more like You. I pray that my relationship with You will be as sweet and as lovely as a rose in full bloom. When my friends and family spend time with me, I hope they see just how much I'm becoming like You. Amen.

And we know that in all things God works for the good of those who love him, who have been called according to his purpose.
Romans 8:28 NIV

QUIETLY HOPING

Sometimes I want answers *now*, Lord. I just don't want to wait. But when I am patient, really seek out Your Word and will, and look for Your help, hard times don't seem so hard.

It's all about trusting You. Once I can get that idea in my head, I'm ready to do some more waiting. To be patient, quietly hoping in You, certain that You'll work everything out someday, somehow. Thank You, Lord, for what You are about to do, today and tomorrow. Amen.

The Lord is kind to everyone who trusts and obeys him. It is good to wait patiently for the Lord to save us.
LAMENTATIONS 3:25–26 CEV

SING A SONG

Music is such an important part of my life, Lord. Singing along with popular songs may be fun, but it's not the same as having a song in my heart. Having a song in my heart means I'm thinking about You and praising You all the time. Having a song in my heart means I'm happy with who You are and who I am in You.

Lord, hit songs and popular singers will come and go, but You will always stay the same. One thing will remain, and that's Your love for me. You will never leave me, never fail me, never forget me. And that's something worth singing about. Amen.

Sing and make music from
your heart to the Lord.
EPHESIANS 5:19 NIV

CHOOSING FRIENDS

Jesus, I know it is important for me to choose good friends. The Bible tells of people who chose the wrong kind of friends and how that affected them; I'm thinking of Baalam and how he was influenced to curse Israel, and King Asa of Judah who made an agreement with a pagan king. But then there are stories of people in the Bible whose friends were a blessing to them—Daniel and his three Hebrew friends who refused to bow down to idols, and Mary, Martha, and Lazarus who were earthly friends with Jesus and let Him share their home and food.

I want to have good friends, and I want to be a good friend. Give me wisdom so I can choose wisely. Amen.

*Do not be misled: "Bad company
corrupts good character."*
1 CORINTHIANS 15:33 NIV

I BELIEVE!

Father, sometimes faith seems like the hardest thing. But there are many other things that require faith. I trust that when I get into a vehicle, I will arrive safely and on time. I believe my friend when she promises she will keep the secret that I've kept for so long and finally told her. I have faith that my parents will supply my basic needs and will take care of me.

The best faith is in You, Father! I believe everything in Your Word is true and that I should live my life obeying it because that's the only way I will have true success. Amen.

*Trust in the Lord with all your heart and
lean not on your own understanding;
in all your ways submit to him, and he
will make your paths straight.*
PROVERBS 3:5–6 NIV

TEMPTATION

God, temptation is all around me. Why does it seem easier to do the wrong thing than to resist temptation? I'm often tempted in what appear to be small ways, but even the little sins can get out of control.

I pray that You will give me power to say no to the things that do not honor or please You, Father. I read of Bible heroes who trusted You and who did not give in to temptation. Their lives were truly blessed. Those who gave in to temptation often had to live with really tough consequences for their sins. Help me to choose right over wrong. Amen.

You are tempted in the same way that everyone else is tempted. But God can be trusted not to let you be tempted too much, and he will show you how to escape from your temptations.
1 Corinthians 10:13 cev

ALL I REALLY NEED

Sometimes I feel like curling up under my covers and staying there *forever*! I don't even want to see or talk to my friends or family. But I'm talking to You, Father, because You understand how I feel—no matter how ridiculous my feelings might seem to anyone else.

Please help me to have courage and see my feelings of low self-esteem as false.

Father, when I start feeling bad about myself, please encourage me with a calm, well-balanced mind. Help me to remember that I am of great worth to You, and that's really all that matters. Amen.

For God has not given us a spirit of fear and timidity, but of power, love, and self-discipline.
2 TIMOTHY 1:7 NLT

DROP IT!

You don't like me to hang on to hurt, Lord. . .for my sake and the sake of the person who hurt me. You want me to let it go, like the dog dropping the bone when his master commands him to.

Help me to let go of the offenses. When my feelings are hurt, whisper, "Drop it! Get over it! Let it go!" in my ear. And if I try to hang on to it, remind me that You had every reason to be offended when You sent Jesus to the world and the world rejected Him. You didn't get offended, though. You did just the opposite! You kept loving, kept forgiving, and kept giving. May I learn from Your example, Father! Amen.

෮

Good sense makes one slow to anger,
and it is his glory to overlook an offense.
PROVERBS 19:11 ESV

SERVING OTHERS

Father, I remember reading in the Bible about how Jesus healed people when He was on earth. He was kind to everyone; He didn't look down on others because of their challenges. He loved people because they were created in God's image and because they were important in spite of their problems.

God, give me a heart of love for the disabled and severely challenged kids around me. Help me to discover ways to notice them and make them feel important. Remind me that my healthy hands and feet and mind are to be used to bless others. Help me to reach out in friendliness to those who aren't accepted by the crowd. Give me a servant's heart. In Jesus' name, amen.

Serve one another humbly in love.
GALATIANS 5:13 NIV

A BRAND-NEW DAY

Thank You, Lord, for a brand-new day! I can't wait to see what wonderful things the day will bring with You by my side! If something bad happens, help me to rejoice anyway. I want to praise You *always*—not just when everything goes right but during difficult times too.

Sometimes praising You is a choice I have to make, and not a feeling. God, I *choose* to give You the praise You deserve. So today, my prayer is that You will keep my heart fixed on You, my thoughts focused on Your promises, and my words overflowing with thanksgiving and gratitude for all that You've done and all that You mean to me. Amen.

This is the day the LORD has made;
we will rejoice and be glad in it.
PSALM 118:24 NKJV

BORING? IGNORING?

It's so hard to listen sometimes, Lord. I just want to tune out my parents when they're talking to me or my teacher when she's standing in front of the classroom teaching us. I'd rather look out the window and daydream! It's hard to listen at church sometimes too.

Would You please help me not only to listen but also to learn from the people You've put in my life? And help me to listen to Your Word too. I need to pay careful attention because You have so much to teach me. Amen.

"Now then, my children, listen to me; blessed are those who keep my ways. Listen to my instruction and be wise; do not disregard it."
PROVERBS 8:32–33 NIV

WHAT AN AWESOME IDEA!

Heavenly Father, I'm so glad You thought of the idea of church. Some kids think it's boring and just for losers, but I'm glad I know the truth. The church people are my family; they care about me and want to help me live for Your glory and get to heaven someday.

There are different types of churches, but the most important thing is that they proclaim Jesus is Lord and follow the teachings of the Bible.

Thank You for the church—it's a place of learning and caring. I want to fill my place and be faithful to come and worship and praise. Bless my pastor today, and let me make my church a better place. Amen.

Now you are the body of Christ,
and each one of you is a part of it.
1 CORINTHIANS 12:27 NIV

TOO MANY TRIALS

I feel like I have too many trials going on in my life right now, Lord. I don't feel strong enough to handle them anymore. Help me to trust in You more and look at my problems less. Please give me Your peace and strength in the middle of all this stress so that my light will shine for You and my faith will grow.

Will You help me to understand what it means to have joy in the midst of trials? I don't really feel very happy with all of this going on, but I can trust that You are in control of all the things in my life. I will trust in You. Amen.

Consider it pure joy, my brothers and sisters,
whenever you face trials of many kinds,
because you know that the testing of
your faith produces perseverance.
JAMES 1:2–3 NIV

PRODUCING FRUIT

Lord, please show me the gifts and abilities You have given me. Help me to know how and where I can serve You best. As I go through my daily life, point out to me opportunities where I can work for Your kingdom.

Help me always to remain in close fellowship with You. I know that if I try to do the work on my own, it will be useless, but anything done in Your name will last. You are the vine, Lord. I am a branch. Allow me to produce much fruit for Your glory. Amen.

*"Yes, I am the vine; you are the branches.
Those who remain in me, and I in them,
will produce much fruit. For apart from
me you can do nothing."*
JOHN 15:5 NLT

GOSSIP

Dear Lord, whenever I'm in a situation where people are gossiping, help me to practice self-control and either keep my mouth closed or come up with something positive to say. I want the words that come out of my mouth to be encouraging and to lift others up, not tear them down and discourage them. Plus, I want my friends to know that I will not speak badly of them when they aren't around. I want to be known for speaking well of others and being a good friend. I don't want to spread lies and hurt others, so help me to think before I speak and to love others with the words that come out of my mouth. Amen.

∽

Gossip is no good! It causes hard feelings and comes between friends.
PROVERBS 16:28 CEV

WISDOM VS. FOOLISHNESS

Lord, please give me wisdom. The opposite of wisdom is foolishness, which is found in going my own way, not Yours. Job tells us that "God alone understands the way to wisdom; he knows where it can be found" (Job 28:23 NLT). I may have a lot of knowledge, but I cannot be wise on my own.

Some of my friends don't seem to care about wisdom, but I see all the benefits it brings, and I can already see the results of foolishness in the lives of those around me. I want to have fun, God, but I don't want to be foolish or destroy the hopes and dreams of my life.

Give me wisdom, God. Help me to avoid being foolish. Amen.

Fear of the LORD is the foundation of true knowledge, but fools despise wisdom and discipline.
PROVERBS 1:7 NLT

KEEPING MY WORD

Lord, I want people to know me as a person who is trustworthy—if I give my word, I'll keep my word. But if I begin making promises and then go back on them, I will give others reason to doubt me.

I ask for the wisdom to know when to give my word regarding something and when not to. Help me to weigh out the positives and negatives first, before committing to something. And then help me to follow through with my promise, even if it's uncomfortable or difficult for me. In Your name, amen.

Many people claim to be loyal,
but it is hard to find a trustworthy person.
PROVERBS 20:6 NCV

YOU MADE ME

God, lately it seems that every time I glance in a mirror I find something else I'd like to change about myself. But then I remember that You created me. You formed me to be just the size and shape I am, and You blessed me with gifts and abilities that are unique just to me.

In a way, I guess I am insulting my Creator when I long to look a different way. You made me just the way You saw fit, God, and You don't make mistakes. Deep down, I really am thankful to be me! Thank You for making me. Help me to be the very best me I can be. . .for You! Amen.

"Bring to me all the people who are mine, whom I made for my glory, whom I formed and made."
ISAIAH 43:7 NCV

THANK YOU FOR LOVING ME

Lord, it's hard for me to realize that You love me even when I don't deserve it. You are perfect in every way, and I am so imperfect! Yet Your love is constant. Friends come and go, but You remain faithful no matter what I do or don't do.

Thank You that no matter how unlovable I am on certain days, You still keep on loving me! You remind me that Your love extends far beyond what I could ever imagine. That's amazing! Amen.

The LORD is merciful! He is kind and patient, and his love never fails. The LORD won't always be angry and point out our sins; he doesn't punish us as our sins deserve.
PSALM 103:8–10 CEV

SHE'S NOT LIKE US

Lord, I hate to admit it, but sometimes I make fun of other people. When I do, I'm so ashamed afterward, but it's so hard! When I'm hanging around my friends, I want to be accepted. So I go along with them when they start poking fun at girls who aren't like us. It's wrong. . .I know.

God, please forgive me! Help me to remember that "different" doesn't mean someone is worse than me. Please remind me that fitting in isn't the most important thing. . .being like You is! So when I see people who are different from me, let me see them through Your eyes, Father! Amen.

"The LORD does not look at the things people look at. People look at the outward appearance, but the LORD looks at the heart."
1 SAMUEL 16:7 NIV

FAITH WITHOUT WORKS

I love You, God. Of course I love You. If anyone asks me, I'll tell them right away. I love God, and I have faith in Him.

But I'm learning that words aren't enough. I can say I love You, but if my actions don't show that love, what's the point? Words don't mean a thing. Even my thoughts don't mean a whole lot, if the way I live my life doesn't match my faith.

Lord, help me to make my faith real. Help me to show, through every action, that I love You, I trust You, I honor You, and my hope is in You. Amen.

Faith by itself, if it does not have works, is dead.
JAMES 2:17 ESV

A HUGE PROMISE

Lord, help me not to worry but to pray when I feel nervous or anxious about anything. Help me to share my feelings with You as I feel them instead of holding them inside and getting even more stressed. I want to be thankful instead of stressful!

When I give thanks to You instead of worrying, a very powerful thing happens that You've promised right here in Your Word: You'll give me peace! And You'll guard my heart and my mind as I live in You, Jesus. What a huge promise! Amen.

"Peace I leave with you; my peace I give you. I do not give to you as the world gives. Do not let your hearts be troubled and do not be afraid."
JOHN 14:27 NIV

EVEN WHEN. . .

I know I'm supposed to honor my parents, Lord. I know it's the right thing to do. But some days, it's so hard! I feel like they don't understand me. At times it feels like they just want to make my life miserable and keep me from things I enjoy.

But Father, I know that's not true. Deep down, I know they love me and only want what is best for me. I also know they're human and they make mistakes sometimes. And I'm supposed to treat them with great honor and respect, even when they mess up. Help me, Lord, to honor You by honoring my parents, even when it's the last thing I want to do. Help me to honor them anyway. Amen.

"Honor your father and mother."
EPHESIANS 6:2 NIV

RADIANT

Lord, I've known some really pretty girls who don't look happy at all. They're mean and sullen, and honestly, most people are afraid to be around them. Those girls may have some skin-deep beauty, but they're not radiant.

Lord, I want to look nice on the outside, but I don't want it to stop there. I want to shine with happiness and kindness and gentleness. I don't want people to be afraid of me or worry that I'll hurt their feelings. I want to have the kind of beauty that draws people to me. . .and I know that kind of beauty comes from being like You. Help me to be radiant today. Amen.

Those who look to him are radiant.
PSALM 34:5 NIV

SAVING FOR ETERNITY

Please help me to be a good steward, Father. I know that means taking good care of the money and things You've blessed me with here on earth. I want to use my money and my blessings to honor You.

Help me to store up treasures in heaven! The kind of treasures I'll receive in eternity for loving and serving You with all my heart. For doing things for others without recognition and without expecting anything in return. Amen.

"Do not store up for yourselves treasures on earth, where moths and vermin destroy, and where thieves break in and steal. But store up for yourselves treasures in heaven, where moths and vermin do not destroy, and where thieves do not break in and steal. For where your treasure is, there your heart will be also."
MATTHEW 6:19–21 NIV

IS ANYONE LISTENING TO ME?

There are times when I feel like I'm calling out and no one is listening to me.

But You are a loving God, and no one is so far away that You cannot hear them. You not only hear my loud cries, You can also hear my softest whisper and even know the feelings inside my heart that I can't form into words to speak.

Help me to remember in those moments when I cry, "No one understands me or even hears me!" that You will *always* hear me and You do care. There is nowhere I can go that You do not see or hear me. I can have the assurance that no matter what happens to me, I will always have a Friend who thinks I'm worth listening to. Amen.

"You are the God who sees me."
GENESIS 16:13 NIV

IF I HAD MY WAY

If I had my way, Lord, every day would be filled with smiles and laughter and happiness. Every day would be like a fairy tale, with birds singing and little animals dancing, and the bad would lose and the good would win.

Then again, if there were no bad things, no disappointments in life, I guess I wouldn't really appreciate the good things.

Help me today to be grateful for even the hard things in life. I know they help me grow. They give me wisdom and bring me to a deeper appreciation of Your goodness. Amen.

God blesses those who patiently endure testing and temptation. Afterward they will receive the crown of life that God has promised to those who love him.
JAMES 1:12 NLT

WISDOM VS. KNOWLEDGE

I'm learning so much in school, Lord, and it's good to have all kinds of knowledge. But wisdom is always better than knowledge. Knowledge is about facts and figures and knowing how to do things. Wisdom is about making good life choices.

Knowledge may teach me how to build a house, but wisdom will teach me to have a happy home. Knowledge may teach me the right medicines to use to clean a scratch on my knee, but wisdom shows me how to heal a heart.

Father, I don't always know what to say or do, or how to respond to my circumstances. Give me Your wisdom so I can make good choices for my life. Amen.

If any of you lacks wisdom, you should ask God, who gives generously to all without finding fault, and it will be given to you.
JAMES 1:5 NIV

THE RIGHT ROAD

Lord, sometimes lies come out of my mouth before I really even know what's happening. But You know what has happened. You see—and hear—all. I know there is nothing I can hide from You and that all will eventually be uncovered. Then I'll have some *real* explaining to do.

So right here and now, I am confessing that I did something wrong. And I am asking for Your forgiveness. I know that talking this out with You is only the first step. Now I need to fess up to those I have hurt with my lies.

Truth will last forever;
lies are soon found out.
PROVERBS 12:19 CEV

CONSTRUCTIVE CRITICISM

Lord, I know everyone has faults; I have plenty myself, I know. Yet when someone points out my flaws, it makes me upset and uncomfortable. How do I handle that, Lord? I know You don't want me to lash out in anger or ignore them. It's just hard to know what to do.

Father, when my mom or dad or leader or a friend tells me something about myself that I know is true and I need to change, give me the humility and ability to change my reaction to their comments. Help me to receive the truth and take it to You in prayer instead of allowing my hurt feelings to cause resentment. Amen.

❧

*Remember what you are taught,
and listen carefully to words of knowledge.*
PROVERBS 23:12 NCV

GOD IS AWAKE

Lord Jesus, my heart is heavy about many things tonight, and I know only You can help—only You can control any of this. You see every side of the story—even when it doesn't make any sense to me.

I'm tired, Lord. I can't fix this. The only thing I can do is pray to You and trust that You will have Your way in this situation. Thank You that I can go to sleep knowing that You're watching over everything and that You're still awake, taking care of it all. Amen.

My help comes from the LORD, who made heaven and earth! He will not let you stumble; the one who watches over you will not slumber. Indeed, he who watches over Israel never slumbers or sleeps. The LORD himself watches over you!
PSALM 121:2–5 NLT

I HATE DIVORCE

Dear God, I'm mad about divorce. I wish moms and dads would stay together forever.

I know that divorce happens and that it's not the kids' fault. But it is terrible to have a family that is all broken up and has to try to be nice to each other in public. I know You made families to stay together, but Satan doesn't want it that way and is happy when families split up.

I'm so glad that You can be there to help hurting families; thank You that You hear prayers and bring comfort. Be with everyone who is sad today because of divorce; let them feel Your love. Amen.

～

He heals the brokenhearted
and bandages their wounds.
PSALM 147:3 NLT

IT'S NOT FAIR!

Life isn't fair. I see so many things every day that just aren't right. It seems like evil wins and nobody cares. But I know *You* care, God. I know Jesus loves even the unlovable and died for *every* person—even those who hate Him. What's fair about that?

God, You are holy. We are not. It is only by Your Son's sacrifice that we can know You. By Your standards we deserve to be separated from You, yet because of Your great love for us, through Jesus there is a way we can be with You forever even though we don't deserve it! Lord, thank You that life is not fair—but You are! Amen.

For the Lord is a God of justice;
blessed are all those who wait for him.
Isaiah 30:18 esv

"FRENEMIES"

Lord, please help me with my friendships! Sometimes my friends act more like enemies. They do things that hurt my feelings. They pretend to be my friend to my face, but when my back is turned they say bad things about me. I want to be able to trust them, Father, but it's so hard!

Whenever I go through something tough with a friend, please show me how to react in a godly way.

I know Your Son, Jesus, went through friendship problems too. One of His best friends betrayed Him. That must've really hurt Him! Still, Jesus forgave him. So help me to forgive whenever people go behind my back and do things that bring me pain. I want to learn from Your example, Lord. Amen.

To speak evil of no one, to avoid quarreling, to be gentle, and to show perfect courtesy toward all people.
TITUS 3:2 ESV

DISCIPLINE

It's just not fair, Lord!

I have to take a deep breath, Father, and first ask for Your forgiveness. Then I need to go and make it right between them and me. That's going to be so difficult! Especially with *this* punishment!

But even though I think it's unfair, I need You to help me be respectful—not to try to get an easier punishment, but because You want me to honor those in authority over me. Thank You for giving me people who care enough about me that they want me to make good choices. And please help me to make better choices in the future! In Your name, amen.

No discipline seems pleasant at the time, but painful. Later on, however, it produces a harvest of righteousness and peace for those who have been trained by it.
HEBREWS 12:11 NIV

GOD IN MY CORNER

I love the amazing stories in Your Bible, Father God, especially where You show how powerful You are! There's one story about huge armies coming to fight King Jehoshaphat. Instead of totally panicking, Jehoshaphat ran right to You and asked for help. And boy, did You give it!

When I come up against trouble, it's so comforting to know I have such a powerful God in my corner. Keep opening my eyes to Your presence as I go through this life with courage and hope while walking Your path and singing Your praise. Amen.

❧

"You will not even need to fight. Take your positions; then stand still and watch the LORD's victory. He is with you. . . . Do not be afraid or discouraged. Go out against them tomorrow, for the LORD is with you!"
2 CHRONICLES 20:17 NLT

GOD IS SOVEREIGN

I've given You my heart, Lord. And Your Word tells me that nothing can separate me from Your love.

Remind me that nothing can get in the way of Your love for me. You are sovereign, which means You have ultimate power and authority over everyone and everything. Don't allow me to be fooled into thinking anyone else has control over me or this world. You are God, and I'm not. And neither is anyone else.

Thank You for caring so much for me. Amen.

For I am convinced that neither death nor life, neither angels nor demons, neither the present nor the future, nor any powers, neither height nor depth, nor anything else in all creation, will be able to separate us from the love of God that is in Christ Jesus our Lord.
ROMANS 8:38–39 NIV

SO MANY DUMB MOMENTS

Lord, many times I say things that later I think were dumb. And I worry that everyone will think I'm stupid. I remember hearing about Moses who had trouble speaking in public and was nervous about doing what You asked, yet You were with him. So I'm asking You to help me be the person You made me to be. I want to learn to be comfortable in a group and to be able to communicate well, but I don't want to constantly worry about what others think. I'm depending on You to help me get it right as I grow and learn. Amen.

My mouth will speak words of wisdom.
PSALM 49:3 NIV

I'M AFRAID

Lord, I am afraid. This situation seems so complicated and scary. It's so much bigger than anything else I've experienced. I get my mind all tangled up trying to figure it out. I feel so much better when I put my trust in You and let You take care of my fears and burdens. Please help me not to fear. Help me to trust You more. Forgive me for my lack of faith about certain things.

Comfort me with Jesus' words to His disciples when faced with a fierce storm on the sea: "Don't be afraid. . . . Take courage. I am here!" (Matthew 14:27 NLT). Amen.

So Peter went over the side of the boat and walked on the water toward Jesus. But when he saw the strong wind and the waves, he was terrified and began to sink.
MATTHEW 14:29–30 NLT

It's About Time!

Lord, I ask that You help me to manage my time better. I realize that in order to grow in You I must spend time reading the scriptures and pray daily. But usually other "things" distract me.

Father, I admit that I spend too much time doing time-consuming activities that are unproductive. Please stop me when I'm tempted to spend too much time on entertainment in place of spending quality time with You.

Your Word says there is a time for everything. I thank You that You have made enough hours in the day for me to accomplish everything I need to do, want to do, and should do. But I know it's about time that I give You time before anything or anyone else. Amen.

There is a time for everything.
ECCLESIASTES 3:1 NCV

A BRAND-NEW HEART

God, I've messed up so many times. Here I am coming to You again with the same thing. Will You forgive me yet again? Will You help me to make this right with the people that I've hurt in the process of my sin? Your Word says that You will, and I'm so grateful! But please help me not to take advantage of the fact that You are a forgiving and gracious God!

No matter what I do, it seems You are always waiting for me with open arms and an overflowing heart. I love You, Lord. Thank You for wiping my slate clean and giving me a brand-new heart to start fresh again. Amen.

But you, Lord, are a compassionate
and gracious God, slow to anger,
abounding in love and faithfulness.
PSALM 86:15 NIV

GO AGAINST THE FLOW

God, You have told me not to go with the crowd if they're doing something wrong. That feels like walking against the current of a raging river sometimes. I can get swept away by peer pressure, or I can take a stand and act in a way pleasing to You. You don't promise it will be an easy decision, but You do promise to be with me and give me a way out.

Lord Jesus, please give me the strength to choose what's right, even if a bunch of people give in to temptation and do what's wrong. In Your name, amen.

Don't copy the behavior and customs of this world, but let God transform you into a new person by changing the way you think. Then you will learn to know God's will for you, which is good and pleasing and perfect.
ROMANS 12:2 NLT

A GOOD NAME

I want to have a good reputation, Lord. When people think of me, I want them to think good things. But a good reputation has to be earned. It's the result of many wise decisions over a long period of time. A good reputation is the result of good character.

Help me to consistently live the qualities that will give me a good name, Lord. When people think of me, I want them to think of You. Amen.

❧

Let love and faithfulness never leave you. . . .
Then you will win favor and a good name
in the sight of God and man.
PROVERBS 3:3–4 NIV

ALL THINGS WORK TOGETHER FOR GOOD

Lord, sometimes I just don't understand. Your Word says that all things work together for good. But this doesn't feel *good*. It feels *awful*. It seems like everything goes wrong for me. I know that I have many blessings, but I just don't understand why You let certain things happen.

The Bible tells me to cast my cares on You because You care for me. I lay them at Your feet, God. Help me not to pick up my worries again but to leave them with You. You are big enough to handle all my hurts, disappointments, and confusion. Work all things together for good in my life, Father. . .even when I don't understand. Amen.

⁓

Cast all your anxiety on him
because he cares for you.
1 PETER 5:7 NIV

THE SUNNY SIDE

Help me, Father, to fill my mind with good thoughts—things that are beautiful, not ugly. Things I can cheer for, not cry about. That doesn't mean I will ignore all the bad stuff. It's just that I'm going to focus on what's *good* in this world—not on what's evil. I want to live in Your light, not the dark. So help me to walk on the sunny side of the street each and every day and to praise You for all good things. Amen.

Fix your thoughts on what is true, and honorable, and right, and pure, and lovely, and admirable. Think about things that are excellent and worthy of praise. Keep putting into practice all you learned and received from me—everything you heard from me and saw me doing. Then the God of peace will be with you.
PHILIPPIANS 4:8–9 NLT

CALM THE STORMS

Calm the storms in my heart, Lord Jesus. When You were on this earth, You simply spoke and the strong winds died down. The waves became still. You amazed the men who witnessed this. Amaze me with that same power in my life, please. It seems my whole world is crashing down. Lord, You know about storms and struggles. It helps me to know that You understand my heartache. Calm my storms, please, and if some of them must continue for now, just hold me. I feel safe with You, Jesus. Amen.

Jesus answered, "Why are you afraid? You don't have enough faith." Then Jesus got up and gave a command to the wind and the waves, and it became completely calm. The men were amazed and said, "What kind of man is this? Even the wind and the waves obey him!"
MATTHEW 8:26–27 NCV

I WANT TO OBEY!

Father, how can I learn to obey You if it's so difficult for me to obey my parents? Forgive me, Lord. Please help me to remember that You gave me wonderful parents and grandparents to lead, teach, and raise me according to Your will and ways.

When I am tempted to talk back, Lord, help me to hold my tongue; when obedience is hard, give me the strength to do what I know is right. I want to honor and respect You by honoring and showing respect to my parents in all that I say and do. Amen.

~

Children, obey your parents because you belong to the Lord, for this is the right thing to do. "Honor your father and mother."
EPHESIANS 6:1–2 NLT

A FRAGILE JAR

Father, if others notice great things about me, give me the courage to tell them the story of You—and that it is only through You that I'm able to accomplish anything of value. Help me to remember that You are the one who gives me power and strength in this life. Anything I do is about You and for You. I really want that to be true of me, God. I want this life to be about Your love shining through me and not about me and what I can do on my own. Amen.

We now have this light shining in our hearts, but we ourselves are like fragile clay jars containing this great treasure. This makes it clear that our great power is from God, not from ourselves.
2 CORINTHIANS 4:7 NLT

STAYING CLOSE

I don't know what to say to sad people, Lord. Sometimes bad things happen to people around me, and I don't know how to help them. I often end up saying too much or saying something that makes it worse. I've tried giving gifts and doing things for them, but no matter what I do, I usually can't fix the problem.

I guess the best thing I can do, sometimes, is just be there. Just stay close and let them know I care. Lord, You said You are close to the brokenhearted. Maybe that's what I should do too. Just stay close.

Help me to know how to comfort hurting people. Amen.

The LORD is close to the brokenhearted
and saves those who are crushed in spirit.
PSALM 34:18 NIV

SEEING ISN'T BELIEVING

God, I can't see You or touch You, but I have felt You in my soul, speaking to me. I have seen You working through my parents and my pastor and others. I have felt peace when I've prayed and forgiveness when I've asked for it. I have seen You answer prayers.

So I just want to say today that I believe in You even though I can't see You. I'm still learning about faith and what it means, but I know You're going to be there for me every day of my life. Thank You for sending Your Son to die for my sins so that I can have a relationship with You. In Jesus' name, amen.

Then Jesus told him, "You believe because you have seen me. Blessed are those who believe without seeing me."
JOHN 20:29 NLT

MEAN GiRLS

Lord, whenever I'm around mean girls, I want to be mean right back. But that's not what You ask me to do. Your girls—and I'm one of them—are not supposed to repay evil with evil. Instead, the Bible says we are to repay evil with good. We are supposed to bless those who hurt us.

It's not always easy to repay evil with good, but I'm going to give it my best shot, Father! No, it won't be easy, but maybe they will learn a lesson from me. And maybe, if I really pray about it, I can win them over with Your love. Amen.

❧

Don't repay evil for evil. Don't retaliate with insults when people insult you. Instead, pay them back with a blessing. That is what God has called you to do, and he will grant you his blessing.
1 PETER 3:9 NLT

ROLE MODELS

Lord, forgive me for placing celebrities on a pedestal. I know they are only people—just like me—but their celebrity status seems to elevate them in my mind somehow.

Father, Your servant Paul told the early Christians to follow his example as he followed the example of Christ. I know I should choose Christian role models who live their lives for You. Even though the world bombards me with temptations and influences of the rich and famous, I ask that You change my heart to desire only Your ways and Your will.

Surround my life with more of You, Jesus. I want to follow You; I want to be like You. Give me godly role models, and help me to become a good role model too. Amen.

*Follow my example, as I
follow the example of Christ.*
1 CORINTHIANS 11:1 NIV

PEACE AND HARMONY

I come to You today, Lord, with a troubled heart. How am I to handle bullying that comes in so many forms? I ask You to give me the wisdom to be kind to everyone and the courage to walk away from people who say or do mean things. Put Your wall of protection around me. Give me Your eyes so that I can see the good in all people.

I pray for peace and harmony—at home, at school, and in our neighborhood. Amen.

There are six things the LORD hates, seven that are detestable to him: haughty eyes, a lying tongue, hands that shed innocent blood, a heart that devises wicked schemes, feet that are quick to rush into evil, a false witness who pours out lies and a person who stirs up conflict in the community.
PROVERBS 6:16–19 NIV

A MASTERPIECE

I sure don't feel like a masterpiece, God.

But You gaze at me and smile. I am Your daughter, Your precious child, Your masterpiece. Give me the ability to do the good works that You have created me to do. Show me Your will and Your way for my life, and give me courage to follow You even when I'm not sure where You are taking me. I am Yours, God. And wow, it feels amazing to be valued by the God of the universe! Thank You for making me, for loving me, and for stamping me with Your approval—just because I'm me, just because I belong to You. Amen.

For we are God's masterpiece. He has created us anew in Christ Jesus, so we can do the good things he planned for us long ago.
EPHESIANS 2:10 NLT

RIGHT HERE, RIGHT NOW

Lord, I find myself confused, unhappy, and lost—all because I have been neglecting You and Your Word. You have been waiting outside my door, knocking, and I have not let You in. Now nothing is going right.

Suddenly I realize that it's not You who has moved—but me!

So here I am, Lord, right here, right now. At this moment, I am imagining You sitting right next to me. Forgive me for being so caught up in other things. Give me the peace, strength, direction, and hope I need to live the life You have planned out for me. Help me to be more loving to myself, my family, and my friends. Amen.

"Here I am! I stand at the door and knock.
If anyone hears my voice and opens the door, I will
come in and eat with that person, and they with me."
REVELATION 3:20 NIV

FINDING GOD

I wish I could see You, Lord. I talk to You all the time, but sometimes I don't know if You're really there. I wish there were a place to go, a place to look, where I could find You.

But You said You're everywhere. When my parents tell me they love me, when I get a good grade on a test, when we have my favorite meal at lunch. . .You are there.

You're not just there in the good things either. You said You'd never, ever leave me.

I know You are there, Lord, even though I can't see You. When I look for You, I'll find You because You promised to never leave me. Thank You for being there. Amen.

"You will seek me and find me
when you seek me with all your heart."
JEREMIAH 29:13 NIV

LOVING MY SIBLINGS

Lord, my siblings are so annoying most of the time! Give me patience with them and give them patience with me. As we continue to grow up together, I pray that You would bless our relationships with each other and that we would encourage each other to follow You. Not everyone gets a sibling, and even when I'm frustrated with them, I need to be thankful that I have someone to share my childhood with.

Help me to look at other people as my brothers and sisters in Christ, that we as Christians are a family who supports and encourages each other. Thank You for blessing me with such a great family. Amen.

Respect everyone, and love the family of believers. Fear God, and respect the king.
1 PETER 2:17 NLT

TROUBLE EVERYWHERE

Lord, sometimes it seems like everything that could go wrong, does go wrong.

Some of these things I don't even have control over.

But I know You're with me, Lord. No matter what happens, at least I don't have to face it alone. At least I know that as I deal with hard things, You're right beside me, holding my hand and giving me wisdom to get through them.

Thank You, Lord, for loving me enough to stay with me even when things are hard. Thank You for giving me the wisdom to get through even the most difficult situations. Amen.

The righteous person may have many troubles, but the LORD delivers him from them all.
PSALM 34:19 NIV

ANXIETY

God, I find myself being anxious about everything in my life. Whenever I'm worrying about things that are beyond my control, help me to remember Your words: "Do not be anxious about anything." I need to tell myself that in every situation. You are present, and You are looking out for me. You have provided for every living thing on the earth, so why should I doubt that You will take care of me? Help me to entrust my anxiety to You, to not take on the cares of tomorrow, and to lift everything up to You in prayer. You will never leave me or forsake me, and that assurance should remind me not to worry. Amen.

Do not be anxious about anything, but in every situation, by prayer and petition, with thanksgiving, present your requests to God.
PHILIPPIANS 4:6 NIV

TO-DOS

Too often, Father God, I find the day's chores and homework on the bottom of my *want*-to-do list. I'd rather play games on the computer, talk on the phone with my friends, or watch TV than take out the trash or do math.

But at the end of those days when I do things that only please myself, I find myself feeling guilty because I haven't done what I promised. Then stress sets in because I still have to do all the chores and homework that I neglected to do and bedtime is looming. And neither guilt nor stress feels very good.

Help me to make better use of my time in every way, every day. Amen.

∽

Good planning and hard work lead to prosperity, but hasty shortcuts lead to poverty.
PROVERBS 21:5 NLT

HEALING POWER

I don't really understand why some people have to suffer, Lord. But I know that You have a wonderful plan for each one of us. And so I trust in You and surrender my worries. I am putting their lives into Your big, strong, mighty hands.

Increase the faith of my loved ones who are hurting. And if they don't know You, I pray that their eyes would be opened. That they would see You for who You truly are—a great and loving God.

Thank You, Lord, for all that You have done for us here on earth and for all that is waiting for us in heaven. Amen.

*He heals the brokenhearted
and bandages their wounds.*
PSALM 147:3 NLT

SEEK PEACE

Girls can be mean, Lord. I don't know why, but it seems like whenever a group of my friends gets together, someone gets their feelings hurt. Then we all end up taking sides, and before you know it, there's an all-out war. That's what it feels like anyway. Things are said, tears are shed, and I just hate it.

I'd like to say I'm innocent of that behavior, but I'm not, Lord. I'm not proud of it, and I don't want to be that way.

I want to be a peacemaker. I want to help everyone get along, not contribute to the fighting. But I don't always know what to do. Give me Your wisdom today and every day, to know how to bring peace to difficult situations. Amen.

∿

Seek peace and pursue it.
PSALM 34:14 NIV

GUARDING MY HEART

Help me to remember that it is important to guard my heart, Lord. It seems that so many people and things are tugging at it. I want my heart to be focused on my walk with You first and foremost, above anything else that tries to steal my attention. Teach me to be careful with the word *love*. I use it too freely: "I *love* this dress!" or "I *love* that kind of pizza!" Create in me a desire to place You above all else in my life. You are my God and my Savior. I love You, Lord. Amen.

Above all else, guard your heart,
for everything you do flows from it.
PROVERBS 4:23 NIV

HONOR YOUR FATHER AND MOTHER

God, Your Word tells me I should honor my father and mother, but what about when they make mistakes or do something wrong? What if I disagree with them?

Honor means "respect," and *respect* means "paying attention to" or having "a high or special regard for." When I listen to and acknowledge what my parents say, I have respect for them. I can honor their position as my parents, and I know I have to obey them.

Help me to understand what it means to honor and obey my parents without losing my ability to think for myself and to always be respectful. Amen.

Children, you belong to the Lord, and you do the right thing when you obey your parents. The first commandment with a promise says, "Obey your father and your mother, and you will have a long and happy life."

EPHESIANS 6:1–3 CEV

STRONG AND COURAGEOUS

Can you make me strong, Lord? I know the Bible says You can! You say that I can be strong and courageous, like David facing the giant, Goliath! But even David didn't have the courage to slay Goliath on his own. He needed Your strength, Father.

That's what I'm asking for today—Your strength. I put on Your armor and take up my sword and shield (my Bible and faith in You) and march forward like a brave warrior, headed into the enemy's camp. I know You will go before me, and that gives me all the courage I need. With Your help, I will be victorious! Amen.

"Be strong and very courageous. Be careful to obey all the law my servant Moses gave you; do not turn from it to the right or to the left, that you may be successful wherever you go."
JOSHUA 1:7 NIV

SHARING MY FAITH

God, sometimes when I read Your Word, it seems to be for people more spiritual and wise than me! But Your words are for all believers, not just grown-ups. You have given me the Great Commission. It's Your command that I "make disciples." Show me what this means for a girl like me.

Give me opportunities and strength to speak about my faith even when it may not be the popular thing to do. I'm afraid I will say it all wrong, but please give me the wisdom and the words I need. Amen.

"Go therefore and make disciples of all nations, baptizing them in the name of the Father and of the Son and of the Holy Spirit, teaching them to observe all that I have commanded you. And behold, I am with you always, to the end of the age."
MATTHEW 28:19–20 ESV

A NEW SONG

Some days I find myself complaining about everything, Lord. I don't mean to, but sometimes everything just seems to get on my nerves.

But I don't have to complain, do I? I can choose to look for the positive in any situation. Help me to see the good in things, even when life doesn't go my way.

You said You'd put a song in my heart if I look to You. That's what I want, Lord. I want to be so content, so filled with Your love that I'm always singing, even if it's just inside my head. Next time I feel like complaining, help me to sing a song of praise instead. Amen.

∽

He put a new song in my mouth,
a hymn of praise to our God.
PSALM 40:3 NIV

LEAVING A LEGACY

Lord, it's so awesome to think that You knew me, even before I was born, just like You knew my parents and grandparents before they were born. I guess that must mean You know more about me than anyone, even my own family. That also means I can trust You because You're the One who designed me in the first place.

Thank You for taking the time to create me, Lord. I want to leave a legacy, to be remembered as part of something bigger than myself. Help me to do that by the way I live and the way I worship. Amen.

The word of the LORD came to me, saying,
"Before I formed you in the womb I knew you,
before you were born I set you apart;
I appointed you as a prophet to the nations."
JEREMIAH 1:4–5 NIV

NEVER GIVE UP!

Dear Jesus, it seems as if I hear the expression "Never give up!" all the time. It's a short saying that I think about when I'm exercising, studying for my tests, or trying to reach another of my many goals. But even though it sounds like a simple thing to do, it's actually really difficult—especially those times when it would be so much easier to just give up. Sometimes I think I just can't make it.

I don't want to give up, Lord. Help me to keep my eyes on You and on the benefit I will receive from finishing well. In Jesus' name, amen.

Let us not become weary in doing good,
for at the proper time we will reap a
harvest if we do not give up.
GALATIANS 6:9 NIV

DOING MY BEST

God, doing ordinary things well doesn't seem like it amounts to much, but in Matthew 25 You promise that those who are faithful in the small things will be rewarded. Does that include simple things like cleaning my room and doing my homework?

God, I want to succeed, but what if my best isn't good enough—or if I'm not really good at anything? Philippians 4:13 says, "I can do all things through Christ" (NKJV), so then I guess it's not about what I can do, but what You can do through me. Help me to do my best for *You*, Lord. Help me to see that the small things are important simply because You say they are. Amen.

*If you do your job well, you will
work for a ruler and never be a slave.*
PROVERBS 22:29 CEV

LOVING MYSELF

Dear Lord, I occasionally find it hard to love myself and appreciate all the gifts and talents that You have given me. I tend to focus on the negative, how I wish I were more like some of my friends and siblings, or I focus on all the things I would change about myself if I were given the chance. I need to remember that I am fearfully and wonderfully made by Your hand—there is no one else that You made like me. Thank You for creating me just as I am. I pray that I will continue to grow into a person who shows Your love constantly and encourages others to do the same. Amen.

*So God created human beings in his image.
In the image of God he created them.*
GENESIS 1:27 NCV

LIGHT AND LIFE

There are so many dark things in our world today, Lord. I know You see it. It has to hurt You seeing what so many people that You created are doing to themselves and to others. Knowing what some kids my age are doing right now is scary. And watching the news is even scarier!

Will You use me to be a light in a very dark place?

Help me to hold fast to Your Word, Lord. When so many around me are living in the dark, let me be light to them. Amen.

Do all things without grumbling or disputing, that you may be blameless and innocent, children of God without blemish in the midst of a crooked and twisted generation, among whom you shine as lights in the world, holding fast to the word of life.
PHILIPPIANS 2:14–16 ESV

NO MORE DEATH

Lord, I wish people didn't have to die. I know that death is the result of sin coming into our world long ago when the first couple, Adam and Eve, disobeyed You. I know You didn't mean for us ever to die. Thank You for the hope of heaven for those who believe in You; thank You for sending Your Son to pay for my sins so that I can live forever with You where there is no death.

Hold me close when someone I love dies; help me remember to bring my pain and fear to You. Give me hope and remind me to trust You. Amen.

"And God will wipe away every tear from their eyes; there shall be no more death, nor sorrow, nor crying."

REVELATION 21:4 NKJV

NOT ALONE

You made me, Lord. You know my thoughts, and You understand things about me that I don't even understand about myself. And since You promised You'd never leave me, that You'll always be with me, I know I don't have to feel alone. I'm always in the company of the One who knows me better than anyone and who loves me just the same. I know Your eyes are always on me, and You always hear me when I talk to You.

Help me to remember that, Lord. I want to feel Your presence with me. Walk with me as I go through my day. Whisper Your words into my mind. Remind me that You are always there so I won't have to feel alone. Amen.

The eyes of the LORD are on the righteous, and his ears are attentive to their cry.
PSALM 34:15 NIV

CONTROLLING MY TEMPER

Sometimes I have trouble controlling my temper, Lord. Things happen that make me angry, and they happen when I least expect it. At times I don't explode right away, but I hold my anger in. Then it builds and builds through other things that bother me, until finally I explode.

But when I act that way, it only makes things worse. I need Your help, Lord. I don't always know how to control my emotions. I don't know how to respond the way You want me to. Teach me; show me how to process emotions in ways that won't hurt others. Give me wisdom and understanding. Help me to respond in love, even when I don't feel like it. And help me to forgive others the way You've forgiven me. Amen.

*Because human anger does not produce
the righteousness that God desires.*
JAMES 1:20 NIV

A THANKFUL HEART

Lord, my heart isn't always full of thanks. I know You tell us to "be thankful in all circumstances" (1 Thessalonians 5:18 NLT), but that is so hard to do when things in my life are not going right. In fact, some things I'm facing seem unbearable at times. And yet, You still want me to give thanks? That's what Your Word tells me to do, but I can't do that on my own!

I can be thankful for who You are and for all You have done for me, though. And I am thankful that nothing surprises You and that in every situation You can make good things come from bad circumstances. Amen.

Sing praises to the LORD, you who belong to him; praise his holy name.
PSALM 30:4 NCV

CARING FOR GOD'S PLANET EARTH

Oh God, thank You for the amazing world You created!

I don't quite understand all the news about climate change and going green. Sometimes it seems like people who talk about the environment care much more about the earth than they do about You. I know You want us to respect and appreciate the world You made, and it doesn't please You for us to be careless about our waste and ruin the water and land. But neither does it make You happy for people to save the trees and forget about You.

I want to honor You by being responsible in caring for Your earth but not worshipping it. Worship belongs to You only. Help me to take care of creation by doing my part wisely. Amen.

The sea is His, for He made it;
and His hands formed the dry land.
PSALM 95:5 NKJV

A UNIQUE PURPOSE

Lord, sometimes when I dream about the future, I see myself doing so many different things—my ideas change from day to day. There are so many things a girl can do and be!

Yet I know You have created me for a unique purpose.

Help me not to worry about the future but to continue to explore this world and my someday role in it. I know You have a plan for me. Help me not to worry about which road to take. Remind me that You know exactly where I'm heading and will give me signs along the way—in Your own good time. Amen.

"For I know the plans I have for you," declares the LORD, "plans to prosper you and not to harm you, plans to give you hope and a future."
JEREMIAH 29:11 NIV

KEEPING THINGS ORDERLY

I don't like chores, God. I confess I don't always have a good attitude about them, and I'm sorry about that. I know that You like things orderly. The Bible says that You created all things and You did it in a certain order. And then You put certain things in place to help things stay orderly. I'm glad I can depend on things to stay in place like You made them.

So, I need Your help not to be grumpy about my chores. I want to be cheerful and not complain. Remind me that I am pleasing You when I obey and when I keep things in their place. And I'm sure glad I can trust You to keep all the big stuff running correctly! Amen.

He existed before anything else,
and he holds all creation together.
COLOSSIANS 1:17 NLT

WANTING TO FIT IN

I want to be popular, God. I know it may not be the right way to feel, but it's the truth. I long to be part of the "in" crowd, and some days I would do almost anything just to make sure I'm noticed.

But it's more important to look for those who love You. I don't want to wake up one day and be popular but not have Christian friends around me who can encourage me to do what is right. Show me the right kind of friends, those who love You. And then if others do notice me, help me to point them to You. Help me, God, not to be so worried about being popular. Amen.

∽

The righteous choose their friends carefully,
but the way of the wicked leads them astray.
PROVERBS 12:26 NIV

CARING FOR THOSE IN NEED

Lord, give me eyes to see the needs of people around me—the elderly neighbor who needs a friend. The little boy with cancer. The lady across the street who has no time to spend with her kids because she's always working. How can You use me to help out? Can I offer to clean? Fix a meal? Whatever You ask me to do, Father, I will do! I want to reach out to those in need as You've told me in Your Word to do. Amen.

Suppose a brother or a sister is without clothes and daily food. If one of you says to them, "Go in peace; keep warm and well fed," but does nothing about their physical needs, what good is it? In the same way, faith by itself, if it is not accompanied by action, is dead.
JAMES 2:15–17 NIV

WHEN I'M AFRAID

Sometimes I feel afraid, Lord. But You said as long as I trust in You, I don't have to feel afraid. You'll be with me in everything I do, and You'll help me and protect me.

I know I still have to make wise choices. I also know that if I'm following Your leadership, You'll never leave me. You'll keep me safe from harm. . . and even when harm comes my way, You'll help me through it. I don't have to fear as long as I'm trusting You and holding on to Your promises.

Lord, please replace my fear with a calm assurance that You have everything under control. Amen.

When I am afraid, I put my trust in you.
PSALM 56:3 NIV

DO WHAT'S RIGHT

I'm trying to do what's right, but when I look around, I see others who are getting away with not obeying authority or following the rules. What's with that?

Lord, help me to remember that You honor and reward what is right and that there is punishment for wrongdoing—even if I can't see it.

I want to please and honor You, God. Help me not to look at others, but at You. Help me to follow and obey Your Word. Amen.

"But look, God will not reject a person of integrity, nor will he lend a hand to the wicked. He will once again fill your mouth with laughter and your lips with shouts of joy."
JOB 8:20–21 NLT

STRESS EXPRESS

Between all the schoolwork, sports, fun with friends, stuff with family, and other activities, Lord, I feel super stressed out. There are only so many things I can do in one day. When I am pulled in so many different directions, I get really cranky. And it's all because I feel as if I am riding on the stress express!

Lord, show me how to arrange my activities, beginning with what's most important—spending time with You. Allow me to take time right now to rest in You. Amen.

He lets me rest in green meadows; he leads me beside peaceful streams. He renews my strength. He guides me along right paths, bringing honor to his name.

PSALM 23:2–3 NLT

ROLE MODEL

I really can't believe, Father, that anyone would think of me as a role model. I'm not old enough to be considered one, am I? But I guess if I think about it, there are people who could look up to me and want to be like me: younger siblings, kids in the neighborhood, children at church. . . Now I need to consider whether my words and actions are worth imitating.

Lord Jesus, please help my words and actions be ones that bring honor to Your name. And if I mess up, please help me to make things right and be a good example. Amen.

Don't let anyone think less of you because you are young. Be an example to all believers in what you say, in the way you live, in your love, your faith, and your purity.
1 TIMOTHY 4:12 NLT

GOOD THINGS

Lord, I know there are things about my future I can't control. I just have to trust You. But there are a lot of things I can control, at least a little. I know if I study hard, I have a better chance of getting a good job. I know if I honor my parents now, it will teach me to honor and respect a boss later. If I eat the right kinds of foods and exercise, I'll be healthier, which will make me feel better about myself.

Help me to make wise choices in the things I can manage, for I know those things will contribute to a great future. As for the things that are beyond my control, I trust You. Amen.

Guide me in your truth, and teach me,
my God, my Savior. I trust you all day long.
PSALM 25:5 NCV

BIG AND LITTLE STRESSES

Dear God, I stress out about so many things, big things like what I'm going to do with my life and little things like homework and social stuff. It's easy to come to You with the big stuff, but it's hard for me to bring the little things to You. But I know there is not one problem or complaint that I have that is too small for You because You care about everything in my life. Remind me that I can talk to You at any time and any place about anything. You care for the birds of the air and the beasts of the field. Because You take such care with those small creatures, it gives me confidence in Your care of me. Thank You. Amen.

God, examine me and know my heart;
test me and know my anxious thoughts.
PSALM 139:23 NCV

RESPECTING MY PARENTS

Heavenly Father, it's so hard to respect and appreciate my parents sometimes. Even though they have given me everything and love me unconditionally, I still find myself annoyed and wanting to yell at them when I don't get my way or am embarrassed by something they do. When I'm feeling angry or resentful, help me with my attitude and show me how to respect them and love them. Thank You for providing me with such wonderful parents.

You are the perfect parent, Lord. Even though my earthly parents aren't perfect, I have You, and I am so thankful for Your presence in my life. Amen.

"Each of you must show great respect for your mother and father, and you must always observe my Sabbath days of rest. I am the LORD your God."
LEVITICUS 19:3 NLT

WONDERFULLY MADE

Father, the Bible says that my body is the temple of God. I guess that means I should stop and think about the things I'm putting in it. I have to confess, sometimes I eat too much junk food! And I also have to confess that sometimes I don't really feel like exercising or taking care of myself. I'm too tired or too busy.

You made me, Lord, and I know You want me to take care of myself so that my body will stay healthy and strong. Please help me to make a plan to watch what I eat and to exercise so that I can do that! Amen.

I praise you because I am fearfully and wonderfully made; your works are wonderful, I know that full well.
PSALM 139:14 NIV

GODLY CHARACTER

Heavenly Father, I do my best to obey You. I know most of the "rules." I shouldn't cheat, I shouldn't lie, I shouldn't misuse Your name, I should honor my parents. . .

Lord Jesus, I want to be known as a girl of character. I want to make the right choices simply because it's the right thing to do, no matter who would see it. . .or if anyone would see it at all. But You see everything, and more than pleasing anyone else, I want to please You! Amen.

"The LORD spared me because I did what was right. Because I have not done evil, he has rewarded me."
2 SAMUEL 22:21 NCV

CHANGING MY WORLD

Father, I want to do great things for You! There are so many people with big needs all around me. Some need financial help. Others could really use my help in doing physical work that they are unable to do themselves. Some would benefit from me volunteering my time in service. And others just need a friend who can sit and spend some time with them.

Please, Lord Jesus, help me to be aware of people in my world I can help. And then give me the strength to help them out—not to receive recognition, but rather to be a light for You. Amen.

Do not neglect to do good and to share what you have, for such sacrifices are pleasing to God.
HEBREWS 13:16 ESV

PRAYING FOR OTHERS

Thank You, Lord Jesus, for the people You have brought into my life. There are many who have encouraged me and taught me great things. There are also those who have hurt me. But You have made each one of them and love them all the same.

Help me to love those who have caused me pain and sadness. I shouldn't avoid praying for them because of how they have treated me. I want to talk with You about them because I might be the only one who stops to pray for them today.

Thank You for hearing my prayers, Lord. Help me to become more compassionate, praying for the needs of those around me. Amen.

I urge you, first of all, to pray for all people.
Ask God to help them; intercede on their
behalf, and give thanks for them.
1 Timothy 2:1 nlt

GOD'S LOVE

God, just when I think things are going to stay the same, something else happens that's out of my control. I find myself fearful of change. I don't want to lose anything or anyone in my life.

Thank You for assuring me through Your Word that nothing can change Your love for me. No matter where I go, You are there. No matter what changes take place in my life, one thing will remain steadfast, and that is the deep love You have for me. When I am afraid, remind me of Your love. Amen.

I am sure that nothing can separate us from God's love—not life or death, not angels or spirits, not the present or the future, and not powers above or powers below. Nothing in all creation can separate us from God's love for us in Christ Jesus our Lord!
ROMANS 8:38–39 CEV

YOUR WORD IS LIGHT

Thank You, Father, for Your holy Word which sheds light on my path. This world is full of darkness. It seems that every day I hear more bad news. I am so thankful that I know Jesus as my Savior and that I have Your Word to guide me.

I get busy with my friends and activities, Lord, and often I don't spend time reading my Bible. Please remind me of the importance of setting aside time for that every day.

I feel so sorry for those who don't know You, Lord. They don't have the blessing of the light that I have been given. Help me to appreciate Your Word and to seek wisdom from its pages. Amen.

*Your word is a lamp that
gives light wherever I walk.*
PSALM 119:105 CEV

MAKE ME PURE

Lord, there are so many messages telling me that it's okay to try the ways of the world. And it's so easy to give in. But You know what is best. You want Your followers to be pure. And something pure can't have just "a little bit" of something bad in it or it isn't pure anymore.

God, please help me to want to be pure. I don't want to do it just to "follow the rules," but because You have told me to be. You don't tell us to do things because You don't want us to have fun; You give instruction because that's the only way that will benefit us the most, and that will result in the best fun!

Thank You, Lord. Amen.

How can a young [woman] keep [her] way pure?
By guarding it according to your word.
PSALM 119:9 ESV

WISDOM FROM OUR GENEROUS GOD

Heavenly Father, right now I come before You to ask for wisdom. Your Word says that if I ask and don't doubt, then You will give it to me. Thank You for that promise!

Please be generous with me and pour out Your wisdom into my heart.

I know I haven't done anything to deserve Your generosity, but I accept that Jesus Christ died for me, and that through His power, I am considered a precious daughter of Yours. Thank You, Father! Please show me the way I should go (Psalm 32:8). Amen.

If you need wisdom, ask our generous God, and he will give it to you.
JAMES 1:5 NLT

SCRIPTURE INDEX

Genesis
1:27. 161
16:13. 116

Leviticus
19:3. 178

Deuteronomy
16:17. 67
31:6. 71

Joshua
1:7. 155
1:8. 13

1 Samuel
16:7. . . . . . . 19, 110
18:3. 84

2 Samuel
22:21. 180

2 Chronicles
20:17. 126

Job
8:20–21. 173

Psalms
5:3. 7
8:3–4. 47
9:10. 68
16:9. 12
23:2–3. 174
25:5. 176
27:13. 18
30:4. 166
34:5. 114
34:14. 152
34:15. 164
34:18. 139
34:19. 148
37:4. 37
40:3. 157

42:2. 57
49:3. 128
56:3. 172
61:2. 63
62:1–2. 49
86:15. 131
86:17. 34
95:5. 167
103:8–10. 109
118:24. . . . 41, 100
119:9. . . . . 74, 185
119:105. 184
121:2–5. 121
130:3–4. 23
139:1–2. 11
139:13. 8
139:14. 179
139:23. 177
142:3. 26
143:8. 32
146:5. 42
147:3. . . . . 122, 151

Proverbs
1:7. 106
2:3–5. 64

3:3–4. 133
3:5–6. . . . . . 55, 95
4:23. 153
6:16–19. 143
8:11. 79
8:32–33. 101
11:2. 62
12:19. 119
12:26. 170
15:4. 60
16:3. 66
16:18. 78
16:28. 105
17:6. 77
17:9. 61
17:17. 88
18:24. 40
19:11. 98
19:20. 73
20:6. 107
21:5. 150
22:29. 160
23:7. 20
23:12. 120
26:18–19. 51
27:2. 43

Ecclesiastes
3:1. 130
4:4. 80

Isaiah
30:18. 123
40:30–31. 89
43:7. 108
66:2. 65

Jeremiah
1:4–5. 158
29:11. 168
29:13. 146

Lamentations
3:25–26. 92

Zephaniah
3:17. 30

Matthew
6:19–21. 115
6:26. 72
6:33. 15
7:2. 53

7:12. 16
8:26–27. 136
14:29–30. 129
19:19. 38
23:11–12. 50
28:19–20. 156

Luke
6:35. 35
6:37. 36
12:15. 83
12:21. 85
19:40. 75

John
14:2–3. 17
14:27. 112
15:5. 104
16:33. 90
20:29. 140

Romans
8:28. . . . . 58, 91
8:38–39. . . 127, 183
12:1. 29
12:1–2. 59
12:2. . . . . . . 81, 132

1 Corinthians
6:19–20 87
10:13 . . . . . . 22, 96
11:1 142
12:7 69
12:27 102
15:33 94

2 Corinthians
4:7 138

Galatians
5:13 99
5:26 24
6:9 . . . . 82, 159

Ephesians
2:10 144
4:25 31
4:32 46
5:19 93
6:1–2 137
6:1–3 154
6:2 113

Philippians
1:6 33
2:3–4 25
2:14–16 162
3:17 9
4:4 86
4:6 149
4:6–7 52
4:8–9 135

Colossians
1:17 169

1 Timothy
2:1 182
4:12 175

2 Timothy
1:7 . . . . 48, 97
2:15 39
3:16 10
4:1–2 56

Titus
3:2 . . . . 28, 124

Hebrews

2:17. 70
6:12. 27
8:12. 54
10:25. 45
12:11. 125
13:16. 181

James

1:2–3. 103
1:5. . . . . . 118, 186
1:12. 117
1:20. 165
2:15–17. 171
2:17. 111
3:17. 21
5:7–8. 76

1 Peter

2:17. 147
3:3–4. 14
3:9. 141
5:7. 134

1 John

1:9. 44

Revelation

3:20. 145
21:4. 163

YOU MAY ALSO LIKE. . .

The Prayer Map for Girls

This unique prayer journal is a fun and creative way for girls to understand the importance and experience the power of prayer. Each page features a fun, 2-color design that guides girls to write out specific thoughts, ideas, and lists. . .which then creates a specific "map" for them to follow as they talk to God.

Spiral Bound / 978-1-68322-559-1 / $7.99